M000216839

Buddhism
From Within

Buddhism From Within

An Intuitive Introduction to Buddhism

By Rev. Daizui MacPhillamy

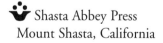 Shasta Abbey Press
Mount Shasta, California

First Edition—2003

© 2003 Order of Buddhist Contemplatives

All rights reserved.

No part of this book may be reproduced in any form except for brief excerpts for purposes of review without written permission from the Order of Buddhist Contemplatives, 3724 Summit Drive, Mt. Shasta, California 96067-9102; (530) 926-4208.

The photograph on the front cover, "The Buddha on a Lion Throne," and the photographs on pages 112 and 116 are reprinted with permission of Staatliche Museen zu Berlin–Preussischer Kulturbesitz, Museum fuer Indische Kunst/bpk; the photograph on page 106 is objectnumer 2207-3 from the National museum of Ethnology in Leiden and is reprinted with their permission; and the photograph on page 108 is reprinted with permission of the Victoria and Albert Museum; copyright V&A Images.

Printed in the United States of America.

ISBN: 0-930066-24-3

Library of Congress Control Number: 2002117541

Dedicated to all people who seek truth.

Contents

Acknowledgements

You just never know in this world how one thing will lead to another. By accident I once heard a song that suggested a way for me to speak about Buddhism in plain English. So, first let me thank country singer and songwriter Tom T. Hall for writing "Faster Horses: The Cowboy and the Poet" (Mercury Records, 1997), the song that got me started on writing this book.

I am even more grateful for friends in the Buddhist world who offered their advice and encouragement. Rev. Masters Daishin Yalon and Meiko Jones; Revs. Hugh Gould and Alethea Waxman; and lay Buddhists Valerie Allison, Chris DiNello, Bernice Donoghue, and Ambrose Schofield—all helped me with the content and style of the manuscript. This book would be in a pretty sorry state without their help. Many others provided me with the encouragement, support, and quiet space without which books don't happen: Rev. Master Eko Little of Shasta Abbey in California, Rev. Master Daishin Morgan of Throssel Hole Buddhist Abbey in England, Rev. Master Mokugen Kublicki of Great Ocean Dharma Refuge in Wales, Rev. Master Saido Kennaway of Telford Buddhist Priory in England, Rev. Master Olwen Crookall-Greening of Reading Buddhist Priory in England, Rev. Teacher Lewyn Blake of Portobello Buddhist Priory in Scotland, and the residents of my own little temple, the Fugen Forest Hermitage. Likewise, I wish to express my appreciation to Rev. Teacher Shiko Rom of Shasta Abbey Press for undertaking the mysterious task of turning my manuscript into a book.

But it is to my late teacher and master, Rev. Master Jiyu-Kennett, that I feel the deepest measure of gratitude. She taught me all that I know, all that I am, in Buddhism. Because this book is intended to be general in nature and not particular to any school or tradition of Buddhism, I have not quoted her as much as I might have wished. But she speaks through me; the ways of understanding which I have attempted to express in this work were developed through twenty-three years of study with her. I bear the responsibility for such mistakes and misunderstandings as may be found in this book, but the credit for whatever is true and helpful belongs to her. Thank you, Reverend Master.

Rev. Daizui MacPhillamy
The Fugen Forest Hermitage
March 26, 2002

Preface:
Why This Book?

What is it like to see the world through Buddhist eyes? How do Buddhists view themselves and the universe? How do they look at life and death, good and evil, the human condition? And why do Buddhists see things this way? What meaning does Buddhism have in their lives? What, in other words, is Buddhism like from within?

By taking a plain-speaking, intuitive approach to the basic principles of Buddhism, this book offers answers to such questions; it offers a window into understanding the religion in a personal way. It is not an academic work on either Buddhist doctrine or the history of Buddhist thought; instead, it is a common sense introduction to how Buddhists think, act, feel, and see the world, and why they do so.

This book was written for four types of readers:

- people who are exploring the possibility of becoming Buddhist,
- those who wish to understand more about their Buddhist friends or relatives,
- students of comparative religion looking for an intuitive companion volume to scholarly introductory texts, and

- committed Buddhists who might find it useful to have a plain-English approach to the basic principles of their religion.

With these readers in mind, I have tried not to use a lot of Buddhist technical terms and foreign words, nor to focus upon religious theory or doctrine. Where technical terms are used, they are generally introduced after the topic to which they refer has been explored, so that they do not interfere with gaining a common sense understanding. Where foreign words are necessary, they are generally given in the ancient Indian languages of either Sanskrit or Pali, which are used throughout Buddhism. A list of these technical and foreign 'key words' is presented in Chapter Seven, often with their equivalents in the Westernized forms of Chinese, Japanese, and Tibetan, which should make it easy for comparative religion students and members of different Buddhist groups to relate the discussion to terms with which they are familiar. I would like to acknowledge the help of Rev. Hubert Nearman in finding some of these foreign words. When writing these words I have deleted special linguistic marks, such as the 'macron', a little line which sometimes appears over the letters 'o' or 'u' in Westernized Japanese. While such marks are quite meaningful to scholars, they simply look strange to most speakers of English, and they limit the range of fonts in which a book can be printed.

The essentials of Buddhism will be introduced, one at a time, as they are actually experienced in the daily life of practicing Buddhists. As the implications of these simple, core observations about the nature of humanity and the universe are explored, they naturally lead from one principle to another, gradually forming a picture of the Buddhist view of reality. A final chapter offers advice on how to get more information on various aspects of the religion, how to locate practice groups and temples, and approaches to finding a personal teacher.

As with any introductory work, this book is incomplete. And being incomplete means that, to some extent, it is inaccurate.

Each of the basic principles discussed in these chapters could well be the topic of a whole book in itself. What is said here is not the final word on anything. And, since one of the interesting things about Buddhism is that it recognizes that no words can completely capture what it is pointing to, maybe that is just as well. At least this way readers will not be tempted to conclude that by the end of the book they know all about Buddhism. On the other hand, if the book has done its job, it should leave you with a reasonably good sense, or intuitive feel, for Buddhism as a living religion. Since it is a religion which is based upon practice in daily life, such a feeling or sense may actually be at least as useful as an intellectual grasp of its doctrines.

I believe that no religion can be fully understood except by those who have committed themselves to practicing it over the course of years. And, for any particular religion, that is obviously not for everyone. If, after reading the book, you feel that you'd like to know more about a particular form of Buddhism, Chapter Seven is designed to help you do that. However, what has been written here is not intended to persuade the reader to adopt my own type of Buddhism, nor any type of Buddhism at all. It is intended to inform rather than to persuade. For those who do wish to undertake Buddhist practice, what follows may provide a common sense introduction to what that practice is about, but you will not get far without other books, and more importantly not without live teachers and fellow practitioners who can show you how to actually live the practice within a particular Buddhist tradition.

I have tried to write this book in a way that will seem fair and balanced to experienced followers of a number of the various paths within the Buddha's Way. Buddhism has been around for a long time, and it has developed many different traditions which look at the world in different ways. This is good, for it creates different doorways to understanding, suitable to different people; it also means that it is not possible for a book like this to please everyone. If it is seen as an honest attempt to step beyond the bounds of sectarian and doctrinal differences and to give readers a useful intuitive introduction, then I will have done my job. Since intuitive understandings are by their very nature subjective, it is not possible to completely separate myself and my own point of view from what has been written here. Therefore, while I will attempt to be fair and balanced, I cannot pretend to be fully objective. Instead, I will try to tell the reader along the way what my own background and biases are, so that she or he can take them into account.

And maybe here is a good place to start doing that. I am a committed Buddhist. As it happens, I am a Buddhist monk and have been so for almost thirty years. So I am enthusiastic about the religion, I follow its practices, and I think that it is the best thing that ever happened to me. This commitment and enthusiasm cannot help but come across in the pages to follow. For me to pretend that they aren't there would be dishonest. When you run into them, just please recognize them for what they are: I'm being me; I'm not trying to influence you.

Naturally, I would be delighted if some readers were to take a greater personal interest in Buddhism and if a few were to commit themselves to the form of Buddhist training which I practice. But that is not my primary reason for writing this book. Another thing that I should tell you about myself is that I respect not only all forms of Buddhism but also all of the great religions of the world as ways for people to find truth, each being good for different people. And I respect the search for deep truth which goes on in many people outside of any religious framework. Since I sense that there is a common core to all of these ways of seeking truth which is more important than their differences, I believe that the honest exploration of any religious tradition throws light on them all. In the end, my main motivation in writing this book is the hope that you may find in these pages not only a doorway into an intuitive understanding of Buddhism, but also that through this experience you may come to a greater personal appreciation of your own path to finding truth, whatever it may be.

1.

Faster Horses

I once heard a country and western song called 'Faster Horses.' It was one of those partly humorous, partly philosophical songs about the meaning of life. An idealistic young man meets an old cowboy sitting in a bar, his face weather-beaten, his hands gnarled; the youngster just knows that this guy has the secret to life. So he asks him all sorts of deep questions about what makes life worth living, and no matter what the young man asks, the old timer comes back with the same answer, "Faster horses; younger women; older whiskey; more money!" Well, I thought, that may not say much about the true meaning of life, but it sure does sum up the problem of human existence: we're never satisfied.

If we don't have it, we want some; if we have some, we want more; if we have lots, we're afraid of losing it. Now, the 'it' can be anything, but mostly the song had it right: it's either 'faster horses' (power, excitement, fame, things which others envy), 'younger women' (which works in the song but strikes me as being a little one-sided—it could just as easily be 'wilder guys'), 'older whiskey' (better sensual experiences of all sorts, and especially ones that make us forget our problems), or, of course, 'more money.' This business of never being satisfied may not seem like all that big a problem, but it goes right to the heart of some of the most difficult things in life. If we're never satisfied, it guarantees that we can never really be completely at peace within ourselves and also that we never get a chance to fully enjoy the simple pleasures that actually do make life worthwhile. How can you be fully present, watching a sunset beside your partner, when half of you is itching to be with someone else, wishing you had your camera, or thinking about how to beat the competition at work? How can you fully enjoy the satisfaction of a job well done when part of you knows that you succeeded at the expense of someone else or have made a product that doesn't really help anybody? Sure, there is pleasure in a new car, a wild romance, a great new piece of music, a promotion; but how long does it last? And are those the things that actually stand out as having given life meaning, when you look back over your life?

By never being satisfied, it seems that we are destined to rob ourselves of the very things we value most: a peaceful heart, true and lasting love, real friendship, the satisfaction of doing something worthwhile in this world. Instead, we seem to propel ourselves in exactly the opposite direction: into fear, anger, worry, and discontent. Why do we do this to ourselves? How did we get into this mess?

No one really knows for sure, but the answer might be as simple as basic biology. Inside our complicated human brain lies the same simple sort of brain that all the other animals have, and that brain is wired to seek pleasure and avoid pain. Now, that works just fine if you're a dog or a cat. Except for those times of the day when you're on the prowl for the next meal or mate, if you're reasonably well fed, warm, and dry, then you're happy; you're satisfied, you're at peace. But there's more to our human brain than just the basic animal bits, and these extra parts allow us to think, plan ahead, fantasize, and the like. This gives us the ability to apply our basic animal tendencies of pleasure seeking and pain avoiding to all sorts of things where it doesn't work so well. Instead of just hunting for the next meal when we're hungry, like a dog or cat does, we are capable of scheming on how to get more and finer tasting food, how to store it for later, how to add to the pleasure with drink and music, and on and on. And, because we are able to engage in this sort of thinking and fantasizing, and because it works—it gets us more and better food than we would have otherwise—we tend to go ahead and do it. All of this is fine, and it certainly has value for the preservation of our species. But it comes at a price: since there is no end to how much food we might have nor to how good it might be, we become so lost in pursuing it that we never allow ourselves to be at rest, and we often miss the opportunity to actually taste, and be grateful for, the food right on our plate. And we apply this way of doing things not just to food but to everything in life.

Whatever its reason for being, this complicated human form of the basic animal drives to seek pleasure and avoid pain is part of who we are, and it's part of what led us to create art and science and all of the things we call 'civilization,' so it's by no means bad. It simply has a cost: vague unhappiness, chronic dissatisfaction, constant dis-ease. Need it have such a cost? I'm afraid so. The reason is that, no matter what goals we set for ourselves using this approach to life, there will always be the possibility of 'faster, wilder, tastier, more….' And, since we are wired as we are, it is very hard not to grab onto those possibilities. Furthermore, our complex brains also realize that at any moment it all can be taken away from us. As a matter of fact, we all know that, if it hasn't been taken away before, in the end it will all be taken away by death. We yearn for something permanent, something we can have, hold, or be…forever. And, since somewhere inside ourselves we know that this cannot be, at least this side of heaven, this desire makes it even more difficult to be completely at peace. So, here we sit: 'cowboys at the bar of life,' right in the middle of a world full of simple satisfactions that really matter, drowning our sorrows in older whiskey and dreaming of faster horses.

Nothing Stays Put.

Now, why is it that 'heaven on earth' cannot be? Why can't we be satisfied with one really fast horse? Why doesn't getting the things and experiences we want give us lasting peace and happiness? There is actually a very simple reason for this: in our universe everything is always changing, always in motion. Nothing stays put. And because nothing stays put, there's no keeping what we've got, and no end to what we might be able to get, if only....

What does it mean to say that everything is always changing? Consider material things, 'stuff.' Things are never quite the same the next time you look at them. That's easy to see with fast-changing objects like a burning log or a rotting tomato, but the same principle is true for things that change more slowly; you just have to look harder. The log will not last forever even if it doesn't burn: in the forest it will break down from the action of termites, molds, and the like, and even if you make it into lumber and put it in a nice dry building, it gradually loses strength and the wood worms and dry rot will get it in the end. You can put the tomato in the fridge, but that simply slows down the process. This book, as another example, is changing, too. The acids in the paper are gradually weakening it; the air and light are yellowing the paper. The chemicals in the ink and paper are moving around and some of them are even hopping off the pages into the air. You can tell that by sniffing the book; it smells like a book because your nose can detect some of those chemicals. And if you did just sniff it, some of what was the book a minute ago has just gone inside your lungs and become part of you!

Really slowly changing or far away stuff like rocks and metal and stars and galaxies change too, but you need special tools to be able to see it because the changes happen in ways we can't sense directly. The same is true for super-fast changing things like atoms and atomic particles: they are too small and their changes are too fast for us to sense directly, but change they do. And, so I am told, Dr. Einstein and his colleagues have discovered that even the things we use to measure how stuff changes, things like time and space, change too. The whole universe of what we call 'things' is therefore really a flow: an ever-changing swirl of space/time/being.

In addition, what holds true for stuff is also true for you and me: we're always changing as well. You've got book chemicals in you now that weren't part of you a moment ago. You're growing older every moment, like it or not. The experience I had in typing the sentence above is now gone; it will never return. I can remember it, think about it, dream or have nightmares about it, but they are not the same as returning to that moment. That point in time and space is gone, and, having been through it, I am slightly different now than I was before. So, we too change: we change in body and we change in mind, and at the end of life there is a profound and mysterious change we call 'death.'

This fact of change is a fundamental principle of Buddhism. It is called the Law of Change; the ancient term for it is 'anicca,' and it is regarded as a natural law, just like gravity. For a Buddhist, change simply *is*; no one makes it happen and no one can alter it; no one can escape from it; change is just the way the world works. Because there is always change, nothing that we have in this world is destined to remain ours. Knowing this, it is hard to be fully at peace. Furthermore, because there is always change, there is always one more thing tempting us to seek after it. And because we do chase after such things, we are never satisfied and never happy for long.

How Unhappiness Happens.

Recognition of this state of affairs—of this chronic dissatisfaction or uneasiness which results from both our desire for faster horses and our wish to hold onto things in the face of a changing world—is actually the first principle of Buddhism. It is called the 'First Noble Truth'; other terms for it are the 'truth of suffering' or the 'existence of unsatisfactoriness.' Both of these expressions are translations of the term 'dukkha' in the ancient Indian language of

Pali, and no one English word quite captures the whole meaning. For instance, to say that the First Noble Truth is simply that 'life is suffering' is misleading, since it implies that Buddhists are somehow obsessed with the painful aspects of life. Actually, the fact that life is sometimes painful is not the real problem. People can handle the occasional pain; it is the constant internal background state of vague unhappiness and nameless yearning that keeps us from being truly at peace. In other words, this First Noble Truth is the 'faster horses problem,' compounded by the law of change.

The 'faster horses problem' and the law of change explain *why* our lives have a background of dissatisfaction and unpeacefulness, but they don't fully explain *how* that happens. What is the actual chain of events that leads to these feelings? Am I, for example, frustrated because I don't have more money, or does my frustration come from thinking that I deserve more money than I have? Do I feel unfulfilled because I'm not a star athlete, or is it because I dream of being one and don't seem to be able to do it? Do I actually fear getting older, or does the uneasiness come from the fact that getting older means giving up the things of my youth? It seems pretty clear that what actually distresses us is the second alternative in these sorts of circumstances. After all, there are lots of folks in the world who have less money than we, but who don't feel frustrated; most people are not famous athletes, and most of them frankly don't care; plenty of older folks are not dismayed by their situation, and they actually enjoy maturity. Of course, most of the individuals who are not dissatisfied by the things I've just mentioned are plenty unhappy about something else. It's not that they are not affected by life in the same basic way that you and I are, it's just that they don't happen to care about the particular things which bother us.

That 'not caring' is an important clue to how the process of unhappiness works: we're only dissatisfied by those aspects of life where we feel a need, where we 'have a stake,' where we are attached to something. So it's not really the lack of a faster horse that's at the root of the problem; the real basis of the problem is believing that we won't be happy until we get one. In other words, it is craving for things which seems to be at the core of the problem, and it causes unhappiness in two different ways. First of all, craving (attachment, grasping, lusting, wanting, longing, desire, etcetera) hurts, in and of itself. To be constantly wanting things that we can never fully have, or never completely hold onto, leaves us permanently in a state of frustration, and that hurts. Lusting, longing, desire, and the like are, by their very nature, feelings of being unfulfilled, of being incomplete, discontented, unpeaceful. Because nothing stays put and everything is always changing, no matter how fast our horse is, we condemn ourselves to chronic unhappiness so long as we hold onto the desire for faster horses.

The second way in which attachments rob us of inner peace is by leading us to do things which cause harm to ourselves and others. Some of this damage is completely internal, such as developing a set of beliefs about how the world is unfair or doesn't care about us. Some of it is external, such as trying to get the raise we desire by unfairly competing with our coworkers, cutting corners on the job to make it look like we're more efficient, or brow-beating our subordinates. The internal things tend to make us miserable in ways that we don't recognize easily. For example, now we're angry about unfairness instead of being aware of our simple frustration about lack of recognition and reward: we have created a whole new layer of misery for ourselves. And, we have given ourselves a whole new problem to solve: the unfairness of the world. Unfortunately, it is not the real problem, and so trying to solve it just produces even more frustration. The external things sometimes work to get to our short-term goal, but always at the cost of creating other forms of suffering in the long run. To use the example of getting that raise, we do things that cause us to lose friendship, lose trust, lose self respect, or have the nagging knowledge that we have harmed others.

This observation, that craving or attachment is at the core of how unhappiness happens, is another basic principle of Buddhism. It is known as the 'Second Noble Truth,' and a Buddhist would say that if one looks closely enough at any form of unhappiness or discontentment, a core of craving, longing, wanting, etcetera, will be found. The ancient Indian word for this core of attachment is 'tanha,' which has the meaning of 'inner thirst,' a pretty good term for what we're referring to.

Is Peace Possible?

So far, I've been painting a rather grim picture of life: here we are in an ever-changing universe, trying to hold onto things that never stay put, always being tempted to try to get that faster horse, never really completely at peace with ourselves, and rarely even able to be fully present to experience the joys that do come our way. But this state of affairs is not inevitable, because there is one thing in the whole chain of events that we can do something about. We can't change the fact of change; we can't change the fact that our brains are wired to tell us that we always need 'more' and 'better'; but we can change what we *do* when our brains tell us this. We don't have to quite believe it. And we are not forced to act on it. We can simply watch our brain produce all of its urgent and tempting messages, and say to it, "No, actually I *don't* need a faster horse, thank you." It is possible, in other words, to do something about the attachment factor: the grasping after, the holding onto, the clutching at. And since that factor is at the very core of the process, changing this one thing can change the whole business.

The idea that we do not have to believe in and act upon everything our brain tells us (or, to put it another way, that we tell ourselves) is, in itself, revolutionary. That we actually do have this ability is easy to see if we use extreme examples. My brain can tell me that I am Napoleon or that the moon is made of green cheese, but that does not make it so; our brains can tell us that we'd like to have all the money behind the bank window, but most of us don't try to grab it. Yet, somehow, when it comes to everyday things, we just sort of assume that because we think something, especially something about ourselves, it's true. We assume that because we want something, we are supposed to try to get it. But when you stop to consider it, these thoughts and desires are no different than the extreme ones: they are simply thoughts, simply desires. We no more have to believe that we need a new car than we have to believe that the moon is made of green cheese; we no more have to seek a younger lover than we have to grab the money and run. *Thoughts are simply thoughts and desires are simply desires: you can believe them if you choose, you can act on them if you choose, or you can simply watch them rise and fall within your mind, if you choose.*

If a person does choose to just watch them go by, after awhile something quite remarkable happens. The individual both starts to recognize them for what they are—just products of your brain—and begins to cease being controlled by them. And this suggests the possibility that there actually might be a way to true freedom and to peace of mind. Our complex human brains may have gotten us into this mess through their ability to take simple animal desires and turn them into never-ending thoughts of longing, but those same brains can get us out of the mess because they have the remarkable ability to step back and simply observe themselves in operation.

When we do this, the law of change starts to work in our favor. One of the things that often surprises people, when they watch their desires instead of acting upon them, is that those desires do not remain constant. We tend to assume that a thought or feeling which we do not act upon will stay with us and that it will pester or plague us until we fulfill it. But that is not what happens. If we simply observe those thoughts and feelings, without entering into them or otherwise feeding them, they rise and then fall away all by themselves. In other words, attachments, like everything else, don't last. Since change is a law of the universe, this can be relied upon. And because they do fall away when we refuse to feed them with either thought or action, this means that we have real freedom of choice about them. If we wish to follow along with an attachment we are free to do so, developing it with our mind and acting upon it with our body. But if we wish to give up an attachment, it can be done simply by using our mind to observe itself whenever that attachment arises, in the sure knowledge that the attachment will eventually pass away, just as a wave does in the ocean. There is even a reliable way to do this; it is called 'meditation' and it is something that will be explored in detail in a later chapter.

People who choose to simply watch their desires rise and fall start to discover another fascinating thing about them. The more we believe a particular craving or attachment, follow it with our thoughts, and act upon it, the stronger it gets. It arises more often and becomes more demanding of our attention. But desires that we simply observe going by, like waves on the water, do the opposite: they come up less often and are not quite so compelling. Over time, they weaken to the point that they stop being a major force in our mind. It is possible, in other words, to permanently give up or set aside attachments. And *that* breaks the whole chain that binds us to the 'faster horses problem.'

How to actually accomplish all of this is a whole other question, which is the subject of the next two chapters. The point here is simply that it is possible. And this is the Third Noble Truth upon which Buddhism is founded: *there actually is a way to freedom from the chronic unhappiness and dissatisfaction of life, and that way is to give up the habit of attachment.* Put in other words, to set aside attachment *is* to find peace of mind; it *is* to live in harmony with how the universe works.

2.
Older Whiskey

At first it is a little hard to understand the way in which Buddhism helps people to find peace of mind and live in harmony with the universe, because that way goes completely against how we usually do things. So, a good place to start is by becoming familiar with how a Buddhist looks at 'how we usually do things.' Then it will become clear how, and why, Buddhism sets aside this usual way of doing things and adopts something much more radical.

First, keep in mind that it isn't obvious to most of us that the real cause for our dissatisfaction with life is to be found in this business of clinging to things, nor is it clear that we could do anything about that clinging, even if we wanted to. Most people do, however, seem to have a general awareness of their lives having a core of underlying disquiet, and a sense that it doesn't have to be this way. So, we feel a need to do *something* about it. But what? Generally, what we do is to take things at face value and believe what we have been told by society: that we actually will be happy if we can get 'faster horses,...more money,' etcetera. Naturally, that is what we try to do.

But this is actually the problem, not the solution. Getting deeper into 'faster horses' does not really help: it only makes us more alienated from ourselves, more unpeaceful in our hearts. In other words, 'how we usually do things' is to increase our level of attachments in order to try to solve the problems caused by attachments. Seen in this way, it is obvious that in the long run this is a really dumb thing to do. Looked at in the short run, however, and without the perspective of the first and second Noble Truths, it *seems* to work. It seems to work because, in the pursuit of the next goal, and in the temporary thrill of achievement or sting of defeat, we forget about the underlying discontent. And when we forget about it, it seems to be gone. It isn't actually gone, of course, and it still has profound effects on our bodies and minds, but it seems to be gone, at least for a while. This basic dissatisfaction in people's hearts, although powerful and all-pervasive, is a background sort of a thing, and as long as we can keep something else in the foreground, it remains so. Another way of describing the usual approach to the fundamental problem of human life is that we try to fill our lives with 'foreground things': things to stimulate us, occupy our minds, cheer us up, and, above all, to make us forget. *Put in yet another way, we get drunk.* And not only do we get drunk, but we try to stay drunk. What the country song said about sitting at the bar of life drinking older whiskey may be more profound than it seems.

The Intoxicants of Everyday Life

Now, to use the word 'drunk' in this context may seem a bit far-fetched, but the similarities between alcohol or drug abuse and the usual approach most of us take to life are rather striking. Let me use myself as an example. I am a drug addict: for many years I doped myself up on 'speed,' 'uppers,' those drugs that make you feel powerful and in control, that make your mind race and make you feel 'alive.' As with other families of intoxicants, there are many types of uppers, and I will not try to describe them all, but let me tell you a little about my personal drug of choice: the drug of knowledge. I am a knowledge addict. And knowledge, as the old saying goes, is power. "I know more than you do"; I have power. And, "I am right." There is not much in this world that is sweeter and more addictive than the wine of being right. Over the course of my youth this addiction deepened and led me further and further into knowledge dependency. There were times as a graduate student when I was so 'high' on knowledge that my mind would literally race to the point where I could barely sleep and eat because of the sheer excitement and fascination of what I was finding out. In fact, I got to the edge of the very 'skid row' of knowledge addiction: I almost became an absent-minded professor. People may think that the absent-minded professor is a quaint and charming figure, but having known some of them and almost become one myself, I can tell you that the absent-minded professor is actually an addict. Fortunately for me, I recognized this in time, and for some years now I have been sober. We might perhaps refer to me as a 'recovering intellectual.' Amusing as this phrase seems, there is a certain truth to it, because the old habit is deeply engrained and the old temptation in the direction of knowledge addiction never completely goes away. As anyone who has had experience with literal alcohol or drug abuse can say, the real question is not whether one is an alcoholic or addict; it is whether one is a drunk alcoholic or a sober one, a stoned addict or a clean one.

Knowledge, of course, is but one form of 'speed drug.' And the 'speed drugs,' seen in Buddhist terms, are the greed drugs. That is, they are the ways of life that intoxicate us through the lure of getting the things that we crave or are attached to. Greed, in this way of looking at it, is compounded attachment. Greed is the use of additional attachments to distract ourselves from the painful consequences of the simple attachments which are common to the human condition. It is the attempt to solve the 'faster horses problem' by trying to collect a whole stable!

Another example of a drug in the greed family is the drug of physical strength. When you feel strong, you feel good; you're in control, you feel invincible. If you also happen to be young and male, you may even feel immortal. Like all highs, it doesn't last of course, but while you're on the drug it totally drowns out that nagging background sense of discontent. So people will do almost anything to avoid coming off of it, even including taking steroids or overworking their body to the point of doing serious damage. A similar drug is physical beauty. You are beautiful, you are wanted; people will do almost anything to be with you. You have the world on a string; you are special,…until beauty, like strength, starts to fade and a new drug is needed. Sexual lust is another powerful greed drug. Sex, of course, can be an expression of real love, but it can also be a major intoxicant. Some people feel as though they are never fully alive except when they are having sex. Like the other greed drugs, it can make you feel in control of life, complete, and fulfilled. But it doesn't last long, and another 'fix' is needed fairly soon, preferably in a stronger dosage, hence our country song's line about younger women (or, as I said, wilder guys). The parallels with literal drug or alcohol abuse are quite strong here. In fact, some people get so intoxicated by sexual lust that they develop an actual clinical illness known as 'sexual addiction.' To mention just one more, there is the drug alluded to at the end of our song: money. And we all know how much value our society places on making lots of money. Come to think of it, Western societies seem to spend a whole lot of time offering us products and services to promote our being rich, sexy, beautiful, strong, or powerful—so I guess we must be pretty well addicted to this greed family of drugs.

The second family of intoxicants which Buddhism recognizes is that of anger. Anger, like sexual lust, is raw emotion, pure energy; you can get high faster on anger than on almost anything else. And it's hard to get angry about something unless you are right, so again the sweet wine of 'being right' plays a part. Anger is so powerful that it will justify almost anything one may wish to do, at least for a short time, and this too is a symptom of being thoroughly drunk. Anger (and its by-products such as irritability, outrage, and resentment) is an excellent distraction from the real situation of a person's life, not only because it is emotionally overwhelming but also because it can be made to last longer than greed. It tends to feed upon itself, and one can thus keep it in the foreground for relatively long periods at a time. If we do that, we tend to behave in ways which frustrate and anger other people, which then gives our own anger further stimulation and justification. In other words, anger has the ability to generate a whole series of additional doses of itself, often without a person even realizing what is going on or recognizing that they play any part in causing the whole business.

However, anger isn't much fun. Although anger feels very powerful, it also feels pretty lousy. And since people, like all other animals, are wired to avoid things that feel bad, we have a built-in motive to try to give up the anger addiction. This contrasts it to greed, which is very hard to give up because it is so much fun in the short term. There is also another factor which distinguishes anger addiction from greed addiction. If people look deeply within themselves for the source of greed, they simply find more greed; but if they get to the bottom of their anger, they generally find something else as well. This is because greed is simpler than anger: it is just the piling up of one attachment on top of another in order to try to avoid the consequences of being attached to stuff in the first place. With anger, however, what one finds at its core is more complicated. Yes, a part of its reason for existence is the frustration that comes from the impossibility of attachments ever being fully satisfied. And yet there is also another part, and that part is usually a pure motive and a positive emotion; often it is love. The love that lies beneath anger is often a love that is misunderstood, saddened, or otherwise twisted up, but it is still love. And when a person is able to see deeply enough into their own nature to actually experience this, it tends to undermine the very basis for their anger. It's hard to feel anger and love at the same time.

Because of the presence of underlying love and the fact that anger is painful to feel, Buddhism regards addiction to anger as being easier to recover from than addiction to greed. Unfortunately however, people often do more than simply feel the emotion of anger: they tend to act on that feeling, and, in so doing, they create vast additional suffering for themselves and the world by actively seeking to harm others. When we act out of greed, we often do plenty of damage in this world in order to satisfy our desires, but at least we are not actually trying to cause pain. When we act out of anger, there is an actual intention to hurt people, an intention which is sometimes carried out with devastating effects. The classic Buddhist texts therefore consider addiction to anger as far more serious and dangerous than addiction to greed, although once a person becomes aware of the addiction, the chances for rapid recovery are better.

The third family of 'intoxicants of everyday life' recognized in Buddhism are the drugs of delusion. The characteristic of these is that they operate through keeping people unaware of what is actually going on, both within themselves and in the world around them. One major family of delusion drugs is almost the opposite of the stimulating 'uppers' of the greed family. We could call these the 'downers.' Instead of counteracting the sorrows of life by producing a temporary feeling of energy and a sense of control, these drugs work by making it seem OK to wallow in our sorrows by creating a belief that we are powerless and have no responsibility for what happens in our lives. Not as much fun perhaps, but quite effective and just as addictive.

Take, for instance, the drug of incompetence or inadequacy. It says, "Hey, don't look at me for an answer; I can't do it. You wouldn't expect me to do the impossible would you? Giving up attachments is just too hard; I'd do it if I could, but I just don't have what it takes." Holding these beliefs, an individual doesn't even have to try to look squarely at life and do something about it. The person is not responsible, so he or she can be comfortable about remaining miserable. The intoxicants of dejection and despair are also in this family. They entice a person into thinking, "You can't expect me to be responsible for my life when I'm down. I can't do it. You wouldn't kick a fellow when he's down, would you?" Again, the motivation to do something about one's life is effectively buried under the delusion that it is impossible. Then there is the drug of fear: "I'd look at life squarely if it wasn't so scary. I would if I could, but I just can't. There are things that I simply can't face." Worthlessness is quite an effective addiction, as well: "Don't tell me I'm not doing my best; I already know I'm a failure. I've said it first, so you can't hurt me. What can you expect from a loser?"

These 'downers' are actually very effective at keeping our minds off of the real problem. Of course, since they do not address the actual cause of our suffering, they wear off after a while, just like greed and anger do, and a person requires another dose. Since they are neither fun nor give a feeling of emotional power, it is a bit of a puzzle why anyone uses them at all. Here again, the similarities with actual alcoholism or drug addiction are rather striking: whether we are speaking of heroin or inadequacy, although the intoxication itself may not be all that enjoyable, at least it is comfortable and it lets a person forget for a while the awful thing which faces them in life. It may not be clear to a person what that 'awful thing' is, but for people who use the 'downers' there generally seems to be a sense that sobriety must be worse than being intoxicated because there is an awful thing out there waiting for them. This can become a circular pattern, since the longer people refuse to take responsibility for their life in this way, the more some part of them realizes both that they are making a terrible waste of life's opportunities and also that they have hurt others. Unlike with anger and greed, the harm done to other people because of this type of delusion is usually the result of not doing things, rather than of doing them. The lurking realization of waste and hurt, added to the universal underlying dis-ease caused by attachment, plus the belief in the existence of an 'awful thing,' results in even more motivation to stay drunk.

Another type of delusion drug could be expressed this way, "Don't bother me, I'm elsewhere." The mental fog of inattentiveness would be an example of this class of intoxicant: "You can't reach me in here; I'm not home. Even I can't find me!" Here the deluded belief is that where there is no contact, there can be no pain. And on a temporary level this does work because, by shutting down one's awareness generally, awareness of pain is also reduced. However, people can never shut down their awareness completely, so some pain gets through, as does a vague sense that the underlying problem of life is not being addressed and that harm is still being done. Furthermore, this mental fog deprives its user of joy as well as sorrow, and many wonderful possibilities are passed by. The great sadness of this situation cannot be completely blocked out of awareness, and the pain of this gives even more reason to seek for relief. If a wandering mind, lost in fog, is the only source of relief a person knows, another type of self-perpetuating cycle is created.

Complete denial is another effective intoxicant. "What problem of human existence?" it says. "There's no inner longing or dissatisfaction in me; I'm completely happy as things are!" Presto: no need to look more deeply at anything; no need to recognize the inner pain; no need to do anything different—so long as one can keep drunk on denial.

Then there is the wine of preoccupation. Instead of relying upon a mind which wanders and is inattentive, here a person focuses the mind mightily on something which will so completely occupy it that nothing else has a chance to get in. A mind preoccupied is, after all, already occupied: there's no room left for recognition of its own dissatisfaction with life nor for exploration of the reasons behind it. "Don't bother me with talk about responsibility and waking up to what is real," it thinks; "this is what I'm dealing with and this is all that matters." The preoccupation can be something which is entirely within one's own mind, and a person may become self-absorbed; it can be something in the outside world with which a person becomes almost obsessed. Whichever it is, as long as we keep focused on that preoccupation, it is what stays in the foreground of our minds and most other things are effectively blocked out. In the long run, of course, a mind preoccupied has the same problems as a mind which wanders in the fog of inattention, and it can create a similar cycle of deepening suffering and addiction to itself.

There is one type of delusion addiction which is much easier to get out of. This is fortunate, because it is almost universal: it is distraction. If inattention and preoccupation are among the 'hard liquors' or 'major narcotics' of everyday delusion, then distraction would be among the 'soft drugs.' Each distraction does not do much harm, but there are a million of them and they can simply take over our lives, interfering with the good which we could otherwise be doing. The most common form of distraction abuse is to go around chattering to yourself inside your head all day long. I personally used to find that when I didn't have anything to chatter about, I'd sing to myself inside my head—anything to avoid being really still and fully present! In addition to using our own thoughts as distractions, we distract ourselves with an endless stream of diversions which arise both from within ourselves and from the outside world: daydreams, fantasies, TV shows, background music, computer games, etcetera.

As an intoxicant, distractions are distinguished from preoccupations by the sheer number of them, by the fact that we don't give much attention to each one, and by our not being particularly obsessed with any of them. They are distinguished from the fog of inattention by the fact that, with distractions a person can tell you what they were just doing ("I was listening to the walkman radio"), whereas with inattention, one is simply elsewhere ("Huh? I'm not sure where I was just then"). Although distractions do not have the same intensity as the 'hard stuff,' because there are so many of them they can make a person just as drunk through constant use. In fact, constant use is how they work: we can simply go from one innocent little distraction to another, all day long, for an entire lifetime.

I find it helpful to compare being caught up in the distractions with being on a hamster wheel. Hamsters love to run, but since they are almost certain to come to an untimely end in the jaws of the family dog or cat if let free on the living room floor, they have to stay in their cages. This they do not like, and they spend most of their short lives trying to escape. To take their mind off of their condition, and to give them exercise and a chance to at least pretend they're running somewhere, people put a sort of circular treadmill in the cage. It doesn't take the little fellow long to find out that he can climb up into the wheel and start running. As he runs, the wheel turns, keeping up with him. Hamsters will spend hours in their wheels, happily going nowhere at all. When I was a child, the wheels were made of wire and tended to make a particular little noise as they went round: 'ka-chunk, ka-chunk, ka-chunk.' I sometimes think of that sound as being the sound my mind makes when I go from one distracting thought to another, never stopping to notice that I'm making a great deal of inner noise, going absolutely nowhere.

Sometimes the drugs of delusion combine their deceptive nature with either the greed or anger drugs into a sort of cocktail, in order to obtain even more power to keep us from being aware of what is really going on. One example of such a cocktail might be blind certainty. One needn't bother with knowledge in order to be right: one can just 'be right.' It doesn't even matter whether this takes the form of idealism (delusion fused with greed) or bigotry (delusion fused with anger): right is right. And when you are 'right' to this degree, you are in control, you are on speed, you have power, and, unfortunately, anything goes.

Did I just say that Buddhism views idealism as a form of delusion fused with greed?!? Yes, I'm afraid that is just what I said.

And I should probably say a little more about that since, when my own teacher told me that, I almost walked out of the monastery! Ideals are great, as descriptions of how we want things to be. Or maybe I should say 'how we *think* we want things to be', since if they actually turn out that way, we often find out that we don't like it very much. But as descriptions of *what is*, ideals make lousy road maps. The trouble with them comes when we try to use them as maps, and then try to force things into 'behaving themselves' when they don't turn out to be the way our ideals say they 'should be.' This is where the delusory aspect of ideals is to be found: our ideals are 'right' and reality is 'wrong.' The greed aspect is found in our wanting things to be according to our ideal. And even anger gets into the picture sometimes, either when we try to force things or when we resent anything that appears to get in our way. So, as dreams of what we wish for and as gentle reminders of what we are working towards, ideals are just fine. To the seriously drunken idealist however (and I must admit that I ought to know: it takes one to know one), they can be an intoxicating source of greed and delusion mixed.

Another example of a cocktail would be the approach to life commonly called 'paranoia.' I am not speaking of the serious mental illness that also goes by that name but rather of the general way of explaining things which says, "My life isn't painful because of anything *I've* done, it's *their* fault." Or, "There's nothing wrong with *me*, *you're* the one who has a problem." Here the mixture is of delusion and anger, and that can be a powerful brew, both in terms of effectively blocking a person from seeing and dealing with what is really there, and in terms of energizing the person into action. Unfortunately, it can energize one into actions which cause a whole lot of harm.

Buddhism regards the delusion addictions as being the most serious of the three types. They are more difficult to cure than the greed addictions because one doesn't even know that one is addicted to anything. And they tend to create more harm than simple anger because they can over-ride the natural empathy that we have for other people, an empathy which causes us to hesitate to do really bad stuff. The harm done in simple anger, while it can be very serious, is usually limited in time and in scope; with delusion driving a person, there are far fewer internal limits and so the harm can be truly vast. Taken to the extreme where delusion and anger are combined, some of the worst atrocities of humankind can be attributed to paranoid thinking, bigotry, and even to misguided idealism. Since an uncomfortably large number of those horrors have been done in the name of religion, this is a topic which religious people of all faiths may find worth thinking about. When our religious beliefs seem to require of us that we harden ourselves against other people or over-ride our natural empathy, that may be a sign that those beliefs need to be reexamined. No world religion really requires its followers to act against their basic human compassion; so if that is what our religion seems to be asking of us, then it is likely that some delusion (either personal or shared) is warping our understanding of it.

I have referred to being absorbed in greed, anger, and delusion as being drunk or drugged because the parallels are so striking. They intoxicate: they temporarily make us forget everything else that is going on inside us and around us. They also lead to a type of let-down when they wear off. And the usual answer to this withdrawal symptom is to have another dose. 'Stay high at all costs' is the addict's motto, and that pretty well describes what we tend to do with these things, as long as we can. Another parallel is that, when we are able to get a little perspective on what we have been doing, we start to see the ways in which our actions have hurt ourselves and others; all too often, since that is very painful to face, we just get intoxicated again to get away from it. Yet another similarity is that it is impossible to get enough of our drug of choice. As a scholar, I could never get enough knowledge. In fact, I never met a scholar who knew enough and was content. I've also never known a tough guy who was strong enough, or a beautiful person who was attractive enough. And is there such a thing as enough sex or enough money? Are we ever finished with anger? Is bigotry or paranoia ever satisfied?

Buddhism has long recognized the existence of greed, anger, and delusion, along with their role in keeping us from looking clearly at what can be done to solve the fundamental human problem of attachment and its consequences. Greed, anger, and delusion are 'how we usually do things,' how we try to solve the problem of 'faster horses.' Sometimes the ancient texts refer to them as intoxicants, sometimes as poisons, sometimes as hindrances. And in some Buddhist systems of thought the delusion category is further subdivided. But whatever the terms used and the system of categorizing them, there is always the implication that these are things which we administer to ourselves unwisely. And there is also the implication that we do not have to keep doing this. Sobriety, in other words, is possible.

The Wake-Up Call

Knowing that sobriety is possible isn't enough, however. Most people won't really try to give up an addiction until something shocks them into waking up to their situation. Generally, these shocks come in one of two ways: either things get so painful that we can't avoid the conclusion that our old ways aren't working, or we get a glimpse of something so wonderful that we can't avoid being willing to drop everything in order to search for it. And this seems to be the way it is for many people who become deeply committed to religion, regardless of which religion it may be.

Sometimes it takes a personal, family, or community tragedy, a severe illness or near-death experience, a disastrous love relationship, brutal poverty, or a mid-life crisis to wake us up. Sometimes the wake-up call comes as the result of an intensely painful adolescence; sometimes it comes late in life when a person looks around and sees friends dying and youthful ideals nowhere close to being fulfilled. Interestingly, it can even come from arriving at the bottom of the cycle of actual alcohol or drug addiction, because many people with severe substance abuse problems seem to be unusually sensitive and spiritual folks at heart. Sometimes the shock comes when a person has gotten to a point where they have committed a crime or have badly hurt someone they love. And sometimes the years of frustration simply build to the point where one says, "Enough of this!" Such people come to religion because they are pushed towards it: driven by the sheer pain of every other possibility.

Fortunately however, all shocks are not of the painful variety. Sometimes a little glimpse leaks into our consciousness of something so awesome and wonderful that we simply have to pay attention to it, and it changes our lives forever. Occasionally these glimpses come as moments of stillness and clarity that seem to arise for no particular reason. For other people, a sort of spiritual call comes when the deep love in a fulfilling relationship momentarily opens up to a universal level. Or, an experience of peak achievement briefly reveals an entirely new and vast outlook on reality. This last reason is why it is not uncommon to find successful athletes, scientists, musicians, artists, etcetera, drawn towards religion at the height of their careers. Another way that this call has come is as the result of a lucky accident in experimenting with drugs. Buddhists generally don't recommend taking illegal drugs, yet it remains true that occasionally some young people who play around with drugs are fortunate enough both to have religious-like experiences and also to stop before they get hurt. Sometimes traveling to a completely different land and culture has the effect of opening up a whole new level of awareness. For other people, it is being alone with the vastness of nature that gives them their glimpse: rock climbers, back-country hikers, and deep-water sailors not uncommonly end up with serious religious commitments.

I can remember the night when, as a young man, I was on a back-packing trip and I spent a couple of hours lying on my back just staring up into the vastness of a starry mountain sky. Something inside me shifted, and for a little while I just *knew* that there was infinitely more to this universe than my own petty concerns, and that somehow I was part of a greater truth. I couldn't have said what that truth was, and it took many more years before I realized that I had to give up knowledge in order to find truth; but the call had come, and nothing short of realizing oneness with truth would satisfy that call. In all of these types of situations, a person is left with the unshakable sense that there is 'something more': that there are truths beyond the limits of the little world they have become used to living in, and that these truths are the ultimate reality. Such a person comes to religion because love pulls them towards it: love of truth, love of love, or love of something they can't quite put into words.

To say that truths are the ultimate reality suggests that there is something stable and unchanging in this world, after all. While things—you, me, and material stuff—change, the basic principles of how the universe works remains constant. Those principles are stable, reliable; and it appears that they are this way because of one particular property: they happen to be *true*. Examples of these principles would be the fact of change itself, gravity, or the fact of desire leading to unhappiness. It is not a coincidence that Buddhists regard the first two of these as 'natural laws' and the third as a 'Noble Truth.' Of course, people's understandings of these things change, just as all understandings do, but the truths themselves seem to withstand the test of time. This means that what Buddhism is offering to its followers is not simply a way to find peace of mind, but also a way to find basic truths. And these two goals are viewed as inseparable: the uncompromising search for truth requires the giving up of attachments (because they get in the way), and people often find the courage to give up attachments (and face the unknown that lies beyond them) because of their love of truth. Some people are attracted to this religion because they seek peace of mind, others because they seek truth; in the end, they meet at the same place.

Whenever people are strongly drawn to religion, they are ready to make major changes in their lives. And they recognize that the only way to do that is for their religion to offer them something that goes far beyond the way of life that they have lived up to this point. All of the world's great religions, except one, do this by looking beyond our universe to a transcendent God, Who is both the embodiment of truth and love and is also the ultimate refuge from all pain. Followers of these faiths step beyond the limits of themselves through surrender to Him, and in so doing find the place of peace and truth by His grace. The one exception to this approach is Buddhism, which finds its truth and refuge in the most unlikely of places: right in the middle of this universe, in the changing flow of space/time/being. It invites its followers to step beyond themselves through becoming one with this flow. But in order for them to do this, it must require of them that they give up *everything* which distracts and separates them from this seemingly stark reality: every attachment, every intoxication. The way of Buddhism, in other words, requires complete and radical sobriety.

3.
Radical Sobriety

A way of life of radical sobriety, which sets aside all attachments and all intoxicants, is Buddhism's surprising route to both personal fulfillment and religious truth. And there are specific guidelines for how to do this: there is a path that leads ordinary people like you and me directly to being one with the universal flow of space/time/being. The existence of this path is the Fourth Noble Truth of Buddhism. The path itself, because it has eight steps, is called the 'Eightfold Path'; sometimes it is also called the 'Middle Way,' or simply the 'Way.' Although these eight steps run directly counter to 'how we usually do things,' they are quite practical and not all that difficult to describe. While a book like this has to look at them one at a time, a practicing Buddhist tries to do all eight of them at once, and so they are more like aspects or factors rather than steps.

I do not want to push our comparison with addictions too far, but I think that speaking of this path as adopting a life of radical sobriety is a useful way of talking about it. There are even a few similarities between some of the aspects of the Eightfold Path and some of the twelve steps of the well known approach to recovery from alcohol and drug abuse. While those similarities can be interesting to think about, I am not going to dwell on them because the differences are even more significant. I will just point out that what I see as the one really important similarity is that, in both cases, sobriety is a way of life free from the bonds of self-imposed obstacles, and it requires of people both that they fully accept themselves as they are and also that they undertake a completely new way of life. The most important difference is in the sheer scope of what is undertaken. The Eightfold Path does not simply lead to recovery from the addictions of daily life; its purpose is nothing less than to take people all the way to the heart of the problem of human existence and to put them in contact with basic spiritual truths. These eight aspects are, in other words, the Buddhist gateway to being fully present in the world in a way which leads to truth, peace, and real satisfaction. Therefore, one of the remarkable things about the Eightfold Path is that it is not only a way out of the addictions of 'how we usually do things,' it is also a solution to the 'faster horses problem.' This is because it provides a way not only to set aside the compound attachments of greed, anger, and delusion, but also to drop away the simple attachments which are basic to the human condition. While the normal sort of sobriety from drink and drugs is immensely valuable, this radical sobriety is *total* in both its scope and its effects.

Its scope is total because the Eightfold Path forms a complete way of life. Everything, from how Buddhists see the world to how they think, what they say, what they do, and even to how they earn their living, is involved. The path of radical sobriety has to be that comprehensive, because if any aspect of a person's life is held back as being a place where desires and delusions are clung to, then that part of the person's life will limit his or her understanding of truth and will be a source of continuing discontent.

The Way also offers the promise of being total in its effects. Yet there is no magic in this. The effects are proportionate to the commitment: total commitment yields total results, half-hearted commitment yields mediocre results. Now, human nature being what it is, there are Buddhists who do not take their religion fully seriously, just as there are people in all religions who are lukewarm about what they do. Buddhists can only be that way, however, by ignoring the major teachings of their faith, because it obviously invites its followers to practice a comprehensive Way that involves their entire being, every day. It invites this, but it does not demand it: the responsibility for a person's religious development in Buddhism rests squarely upon their own shoulders.

The word that is used to describe the promised effect of this Path of radical sobriety is 'enlightenment,' and it is a word that is notoriously hard to define. Since it is the alternative to a life of attachment and intoxication, it obviously must have something to do with the complete cessation of all forms of grasping and delusion, and also with living in harmony with the truth of 'things as they really are,' including their changeable nature. But what is that actually like? Over the centuries, writers have tried various ways of describing it, and some of these will be examined in more detail later, but the one thing that they all agree upon is that no description is really adequate or accurate. That is because enlightenment is not a state or an experience; rather, *it is an entire way of being*, and it is a way of being that requires of people (among other things) that they give up the very thinking about things which is the basis of talking about anything. That is a problem for a book like this, since all a book can do is talk about things. Nonetheless, if I don't even try to talk about it, there is not much point in mentioning the Eightfold Path at all. While enlightenment itself may be ultimately indescribable, words can at least point in its general direction, and that seems worth doing. Such words are sometimes described in Buddhism as 'a finger pointing at the moon,' with the moon being enlightenment itself. What follows are a bunch of such words; please just don't mistake this 'finger' for the 'moon.'

Enlightenment is said to be unborn and undying, eternal and changeless, simultaneously empty of all things and totally full, the ultimate happiness and at the same time calm and even-minded, filled with a love and a compassion which are awe-full, wise within unknowing, consciousness unbounded and unfettered. It has been compared to awakening from a long dream, returning home, being released from prison, or becoming sober from a life-long drunk. From these descriptions it is plain to see that, whatever enlightenment actually is, it involves both the end of dissatisfaction and the finding of ultimate truths. As such, it unites people who have come to Buddhism because of the 'push' of suffering with those who have come out of the 'pull' of love for truth.

The reason for this remarkable union is that, in the Buddhist way of doing things, the cessation of suffering and the finding of ultimate truths both happen to require the same thing: giving up all attachments, including all forms of intoxication. Enlightenment is another word for what happens when all of these are dropped away. The reason why giving up all attachments is necessary in order to find freedom from suffering was explained in the Second and Third Noble Truths mentioned in the first chapter. The reason why giving up all attachments is required for drawing near to ultimate truths is because attachment sets into motion complicated chains of cause and effect that distort our natural abilities to see and understand what is really there. How attachment does this, and how the chains of cause and effect work, is described in detail in a fascinating area of Buddhist teaching known as 'dependent origination' or 'conditioned coproduction' ('paticca samuppada' in the Pali language), a topic which lies beyond the scope of this book but which you might enjoy looking up elsewhere.

In view of how total the scope of enlightenment is, it is somewhat surprising that its outward signs are not all that spectacular. They are simple yet unbounded charity, tenderness, benevolence, and empathy. The person who dwells within enlightenment does not appear unusual, special, or different. Such people are, on the contrary, both ordinary and plain, yet there is something about them which makes a person want to be around them. This 'dwelling within enlightenment' is not something which is all that uncommon.

Admittedly, it has always been rare to have enlightenment as one's permanent state of being, to have all attachments permanently given up, all illusions permanently dissolved. Such a person is said to have realized complete enlightenment (or 'nirvana,' a term that will be discussed more in Chapter 6) and is sometimes called an 'arahant,' a 'fully awakened one.' But many are those who have managed to set aside the bonds of desire and addiction long enough to experience a good, full taste of enlightenment. Such people are called 'stream enterers,' and one such taste is enough to revolutionize their lives. Continuing onward along the Path, such tastes become more frequent and deep, and so does a person's commitment to go even further. The fortunate side of this is that it means that the truly serious Buddhist is amply satisfied in his or her search for truth and peace, long before reaching the point of nirvana. The unfortunate side is that it also means that the word 'enlightenment' gets used for all sorts of different things, ranging from the first brief taste to the complete enlightenment of nirvana, and this causes lots of confusion. But that is just the way things are, and a little verbal confusion is a small price to pay for recognizing the fact that enlightenment is not restricted to only the most advanced practitioners of the religion.

One might ask why different words are not used to refer to these different types of enlightenment. As a matter of fact, sometimes they are, but not generally. And with good reason, I think. The problem with using various terms for enlightenment is that there actually aren't 'different types of enlightenment.' Whatever it may be, enlightenment is one and undivided: a little taste is as much enlightenment as the full and permanent thing. And, at another level, the confusion caused by using just one term for enlightenment is usually resolved by the course of ongoing Buddhist training. This is because *enlightenment is inseparable from the process of training itself:* even the arahant (or perhaps I should say "especially the arahant") continues to practice the eight aspects of the Way every moment of the day, every day of his or her life. Ultimately then, *enlightenment is the Path and the Path is enlightenment.* This explains why Buddhism places so much importance on the eight aspects of the Path of radical sobriety.

Aspect One: Understanding Things as They Are

A certain amount of understanding of 'things as they are' is the beginning of the Eightfold Path. Unless a person has some degree of awareness of how Buddhism views the way the world works, there is no reason for him or her to seek truth nor to undertake the hard work of becoming radically sober. So, while the other seven aspects are undertaken simultaneously, at least some progress in this one must be made first, in order to open the door to the rest.

There are only a few basic things which a Buddhist needs to understand in order to get started. The first one is that there really is a fundamental problem with life as we usually live it. To continue our addiction metaphor, the first step is to admit to oneself that one actually *is* an addict and that everything one has done thus far to fix things has not worked: a whole new way of life is required. It is interesting that this is also the first step in recovery from substance abuse. In other words, unless the things which have been described up to this point in the book resonate with a person at least to some extent, then the whole rest of Buddhist training will simply not make sense and will seem pointless. This understanding of the human condition is what was described in the first chapter as the First Noble Truth: faster horses, younger women, older whiskey, and more money don't really bring lasting happiness.

Having some appreciation of the Second Noble Truth is another of the aspects of this step on the Path. In order to go forward with the rest of the 'recovery program,' there has to be some grasp of the principle that the cause for fundamental frustration and suffering lies in the fact that we hold onto things, grasp after them, are attached to them.

And there has to be some measure of belief that there is actually something we can do about all this. We can't stop the way the world works (although much of what we usually do under the influence of greed, anger, or delusion seems to be an attempt to do just that), but we can change how we relate to it: we can give up our grabbing onto things and accept life as it actually is. Then peace, contentment, and real happiness will arise naturally. This is the third of the Noble Truths we have been talking about. And the Eightfold Path itself, which is the fourth Noble Truth, also has to be understood to some degree in order to be practiced. These four Noble Truths are the core and essence of Buddhism; they are the very things which lead all the way to enlightenment. So some understanding of them is essential in order for Buddhist practice to take place.

But how does a person get to such an understanding? For some people, it starts as a matter of belief. The Buddhist texts and teachers say that the Noble Truths describe how the world works, and one simply takes them at their word. However, that is not the only way in which the Noble Truths can be understood. In fact, belief alone is not capable of producing the necessary level of understanding. This is because, if a person's insight into them stays only at the level of belief, they are simply a notion in the person's head, and this is not enough reason for someone to undertake the hard work of following the Eightfold Path in earnest. At some point the Noble Truths have to be actually *experienced* as being true in order for the necessary level of commitment to occur. That experience can be with the mind or with the heart. With the mind, it is a matter of deep personal conviction of the truth of what they teach, based upon personal knowledge. With the heart, it can be an intuitive feeling, a deep faith, or even a direct perception of their reality. Some people actually *see* them in operation, moment by moment; for others, initial belief grows into an abiding faith which carries them onward in their practice of the Path.

So, while belief is one starting point, it is not the only one. An unusual characteristic of Buddhism as a religion is that it does not require its adherents to believe anything. Instead, it teaches that the Way is to be experienced, to be tried out and tested in life, and to be accepted or rejected on the basis of its fruits in actual practice. Because of this, Buddhists, particularly those in the West who have come to it with a scientific or other background which is skeptical of belief, are able to undertake the Eightfold Path provisionally. Some come to it because it makes sense intellectually and adopt it as a working hypothesis; then they see over time whether or not it actually leads in the direction it promises. Others come to it because of its intuitive appeal, and then either stay with it or not depending upon the results of their Buddhist training. As with a beginning belief, these initial levels of intellectual or intuitive understanding, along with the provisional commitment that goes with them, must deepen with time and experience if a person is to continue in the Buddhist Way.

Things as far reaching as the Four Noble Truths cannot be understood at a deep level quickly. It is only through following the rest of the Eightfold Path over the course of time that people come to a profound, direct, and personal experience of their world in the manner which is described by the Noble Truths. This deepening of understanding not only makes it possible to go onward on the Path; it also makes it increasingly easy to stop intoxicating oneself and to let go of the habits of attachment. And with this, acceptance of 'just what is' arises naturally. Acceptance in Buddhism is not something that one has to find or 'make happen': it is simply the natural consequence of deep understanding. And from acceptance comes serenity.

These are some of the reasons why this first aspect of the Eightfold Path is so important. Buddhists generally call it the step of 'right understanding.'

Aspect Two: Clear Thinking

While thought alone is not sufficient to bring about deep understanding, its role is nonetheless important. It can work powerfully either for or against the process of enlightenment. For this reason, the second facet of the Path is 'right thought.' Now, it is fairly obvious that thought can work against liberation because many of the intoxicants mentioned in the previous chapter are types of misguided thinking: constant inner chatter, paranoid views, fixed notions that one is incompetent, and the obsession with collecting knowledge are just a few examples. The opposite is equally true: thoughts which help a person to set aside their attachments and intoxications will be useful to people in strengthening their commitment and in guiding them in their practice of the Way.

How does Buddhism recommend setting aside intoxicating and misleading thoughts and undertaking helpful ones? There are several ways, but before describing them it might be good to mention one way which is *not* recommended. That way is to brainwash oneself: to forcibly replace one way of thinking about the world with another. No matter how foolish the first way may be, nor how wise its replacement may be, the act of forcing oneself is itself unwise and doomed to failure. Some schools of Buddhism (including my own) would say that this is because there is within each of us something which deeply loves truth and is already attuned to it. This 'something,' which is variously called 'Buddha Nature,' 'bodhicitta,' or 'the Mind that seeks the Way,' may not be accessible to our conscious mind, but it is there nonetheless. It is what guides a person onwards in his or her religious training, even without knowing that it is there. And its nature is fundamentally different from the harsh, judgmental, and superficially certain mind with which one attempts to brainwash oneself. Indeed, Buddha Nature cannot be brainwashed, and it will resist any attempt to do so, even one which is well intentioned. Therefore, the attempt to forcibly replace one way of thinking with another will ultimately run afoul of this deep inner sense of truth, and the results of such a misguided effort will be unstable.

One of the truly useful ways for individuals to change their type of thinking is simply through study. People find it helpful to read the classic texts and commentaries that form the core teachings of their branch of the religion. Some do this because they find that these teachings simply make sense, and this good sense acts to dispel their habitual views. Others do it because reading the teachings, known collectively as 'Dharma,' seems to cause something to 'sink in' in an indefinable way, a way which, over time, results in new types of thinking about the world. Dharma study, because there is no forcing involved, helps rather than hinders the work of that inner Buddha Nature.

Another way is to honestly question the things we tell ourselves. There is a place in Buddhist training for constructive doubt. Another one of the unusual aspects of Buddhism as a religion is its willingness, even its insistence, upon allowing questions to arise about everything, including what it teaches. This honest questioning is so much a part of some forms of Buddhist practice that there is a saying in the Zen school, "Great doubt—great understanding; little doubt—little understanding." Constructive doubt is questioning with a mind which seeks nothing more than truth and is open to all possibilities, simply posing the question, "Is this true?" That is quite different from the destructive form of doubt which actually does not take the form of a question at all. It says, in effect, "I don't believe it; prove it!"

The process of asking constructive questions, of being inwardly honest about the truth of our ideas, is helped along by two of the other aspects of the path, mindfulness and meditation, which will be explored later. These aspects are relevant here, though, because they also interact with the thought aspect in another way: they undermine our dependence upon thinking as our sole way of knowing. Unhelpful, intoxicating thoughts tend to have a large effect upon us because we generally rely upon our ideas to act as a road map for how to live our lives. But it turns out that these maps are not as accurate as we might wish, even when the thoughts are well tested for truth, much less when they are not. Fortunately, there are other ways of knowing truth besides thinking, and the Path aspects of mindfulness and meditation help to develop those alternative means. When there is no need to rely solely upon thinking to make one's way through life, one can afford to do less of it. Doing less of it means that there is less chance for distracting and inaccurate thoughts to get up to mischief. And that is a large part of right thought.

Many Buddhists find that when they stop filling their minds with their habitual distracting and delusive thoughts, an interesting thing happens. Other thoughts, which have always been there but have rarely had a chance to be heard over the constant 'ka-chunk, ka-chunk, ka-chunk' of the hamster wheel, come to the forefront: thoughts involving selfless generosity, compassion, love, and empathy. Some forms of Buddhism simply allow this process to happen naturally; other forms encourage it with formal practices in which this direction of thought is gently developed and extended in a regular and systematic manner. Whichever way these thoughts arise, they are regarded as aspects of enlightenment itself. And that, to a Buddhist, is important.

Aspect Three: Taking Care with Speech

The aspects of right understanding and right thought refer to a person's inner life, to things that go on inside the mind. The next three steps are about actions that someone can take in the world. One reason that the scope of the Eightfold Path is so comprehensive is that it invites a person to work at both levels at once: from the inside outward into action, and from action inward into one's state of being. How a person is, and what a person does, are inseparable, so this approach makes sense; both sides complement and reinforce each other.

The first of the three outward-looking Path factors centers on what a person says. Truthfulness is a major part of this. If a person is seriously concerned about finding and living by truth, then it follows that he or she can hardly afford to go around knowingly misleading others. The hypocrisy of that would simply be too painful. Truth is valued by Buddhists both in the sense of 'absence of falsehood' and in the sense of 'reality.' As absence of falsehood, living within truth is sobriety itself: it is our natural state, which is present when the falsehoods of various intoxications and distractions are removed. Truth as reality is a positive goal of Buddhist training: to live within it is to be, ever more closely, one with what *is*. In this sense, truth and enlightenment are intimately related. When a Buddhist understands that the essence of his or her religious practice is to set aside both falsehoods and the attachments which are based upon them, it becomes unbearable to speak falsely. When one stops to reflect upon it, this is all fairly obvious; but because we are human and our old, habitual ways of relating to each other are strong, Buddhism makes a point of reminding people of the importance of taking care with the truthfulness of our speech.

In addition to speaking truthfully, there are several other sides to taking care with words. 'Right speech,' as this aspect of the Path is often called, also includes attempting to speak both in ways that avoid doing harm and in ways that are of positive benefit. Truthfulness is a factor in both of these, of course, but it is not the only factor. Harmful speech includes not only falsehoods but also speech that is harsh, demeaning, judgmental, angry, cynical, and the like. If we value, as a basic goal of our religious practice, helping all people find peace of mind and inner contentment, it doesn't make much sense for us to deliberately use words which not only cause our listeners fear, anger, or distress but which also intoxicate ourselves with anger or delusion in the process. Often people talk in harsh ways not because it is their wish to do harm, but rather because they believe that this sort of speech is the only way to deal with difficult situations. Buddhism suggests, however, that this is not true; gentle and loving words will get through to people better than any other form of speech, in those circumstances where words can get through at all. This last phrase is important, and it points to another basic characteristic of the

Buddhist way of seeing the world: learning to accept things as they are and realizing that there are limits upon our ability to make things the way we want them to be. This all-acceptance is not passive resignation, but rather it is an active and positive consequence of both letting go of attachments and of seeing things more clearly for how they are.

One of the properties of 'how things are' is that there are quite a number of things which we can't do much about. It is usually in this sort of situation that, in frustration, we try to force other people to 'behave themselves' through the use of various weapons, including verbal ones. This, however, rarely succeeds and usually just makes matters worse. This is because an individual who receives a hostile, critical, or belittling communication usually hears the attack more clearly than the information being conveyed within it. The sense of being attacked brings up feelings of hurt and a desire to either escape or take defensive action. And the actions of escape or defense block out much of what the other person was actually trying to communicate. The same information, conveyed in a gentle and loving way, does not incite a person to flee or raise defensive shields. So, it will stand the best chance of getting through, if anything will. This part of right speech is, therefore, not simply about being nice to people; it is also about being truly effective.

Taking care with speech also includes speaking in ways which will actually benefit others. There is plenty of talk which is neither untruthful nor hurtful but which also does no particular good: this is 'idle talk.' When this sort of talk helps people relax and get to know one another, then it opens the way to more useful things and it really does have a beneficial use; it is actually a form of right speech. But it often serves a different purpose entirely: it is a way of sharing the intoxicant of distraction. Participating in idle chatter is sort of like passing the bottle of distraction back and forth, with everyone getting tipsy. In that case, abstaining from indulging it is part of the path of radical sobriety.

When people start looking at what they say with an ear to whether or not it really serves a good purpose, they tend to find that a great deal of what they talk about fails to meet this test. This explains why, when Buddhists gather together for religious retreats, they tend to be a rather quiet bunch.

The practice of taking care to speak only in ways that are truthful, compassionate, and useful has effects which go far beyond the realm of verbal interactions between people. First of all, talk is what we use to agree upon action, so the way we talk about things is bound to have significant consequences for what we do about them. Secondly, since many people think in words—since thoughts are often a form of inner speech—our habits of speech and our habits of thought are very closely connected. And it is those thoughts which influence our entire view of the world, for better or worse.

For all of these reasons, the Path aspect of right speech, while it may seem fairly minor at first glance, has an honored place among the eight types of practice which lead the Buddhist towards enlightenment.

Aspect Four: Taking Care with Actions

This aspect of the Eightfold Path, taking care with what we do, covers a lot of ground, and various types of Buddhism divide this territory up somewhat differently. There are some common principles, however, which are considered so clear and so important that they are generally accepted by all major schools of Buddhism; it is these that are considered in this section.

1. It is pretty clear that a person who is intent upon living a life of truth and harmony cannot afford to deprive others of the same opportunity by taking away their life. That one must refrain from killing other people is so plain to see that almost all of the major religions of the world have it as a basic precept. It is also evident from experience that people who violate this principle deprive

themselves of peace of mind for a very long time. A Buddhist might understand this fact as being caused by an intuitive bond of empathy which connects all people, and therefore killing, which does the ultimate violence to another person, does incredible damage to oneself as well. While the damage is not completely irreparable (since all things are subject to change), it is nonetheless massive and to be avoided if at all possible. The same principle holds true for depriving oneself of the opportunity to continue towards enlightenment in this life by committing suicide. Accordingly, both murder and suicide are regarded by many Buddhists as among the most serious mistakes they could make.

The principle of not taking life becomes a bit less clear to understand, and correspondingly more uncomfortable to apply, when it comes to situations that are more complex than murder and suicide. Actually, suicide itself is sometimes more complex than it looks, particularly when someone considering it is terminally ill and facing almost inevitable grave disability. Most Buddhists would still consider the taking of one's own life under these circumstances to be unwise, as such an act assumes that nothing of value can be learned through the experience of terminal illness and that the ill person has nothing left to offer to the world. As both of these assumptions are highly questionable, suicide under even these circumstances is discouraged.

But it is not condemned, because another interesting feature of the Buddhist religion is that it has no concept of sin. All of the unwise actions discussed in this chapter are held to be mistakes—and something like murder is a huge mistake—but mistakes are simply very sad: they do not require condemnation. This explains a few things which appear quite paradoxical in how Buddhists behave. In the case of suicide, for example, a monk or teacher may try vigorously to dissuade someone from killing themself and then turn around after the person commits suicide and give them the largest type of memorial service in the liturgy. Such a service is celebrated on the assumption that the deceased person (and their relatives) can use all the help they can get, and since there is no condemnation of that person, there is no reason not to give such help.

Another complexity occurs when the question arises of whether or not the taking of life is acceptable when sanctioned by law. Many Buddhists feel that it is not, and they oppose such things as capital punishment on the grounds that it simply compounds one tragedy with another, failing to set anything right, and that it ignores the concept of universal change, denying the possibility that a hardened criminal may yet have a positive offering to make to the world.

But what about the killing which occurs as a result of military or police action? Here adherents of Buddhism are more divided, with some adopting a pacifist position and others maintaining that sometimes even something as horrible as warfare may be necessary in order to prevent an even greater tragedy.

This latter type of position, that a basic precept may need to be broken in order to prevent a greater harm or promote a greater good, is often encountered in Buddhist ethics. It is not simply reserved for discussions of killing, but is applied throughout the guidelines for life provided by the Eightfold Path. The various ethical principles set forth by the Path are not generally regarded as absolute rules. Instead, they are seen as descriptions of behaviors which accord with the Way: descriptions, in other words, of what it is like to live within enlightenment. Seen like this, they tend to be applied not as rigid moral directives but rather as proven means to fostering the greater good of a peaceful and satisfying life for everyone. This greater good, and its corresponding principle of avoiding a greater harm, is used as a standard, both for the interpretation of various specific ethical guidelines and also in those inevitable cases where one guideline conflicts with another.

This approach allows great flexibility in Buddhist ethics, and it also places the responsibility for one's actions squarely upon the shoulders of each individual. However, everything has its plus side and its minus side, and the principle of promoting a greater good or avoiding a greater harm can be abused to justify doing all manner of unwise things. Unfortunately, in the history of Buddhism that has sometimes occurred. Some of the leaders of my own school of Buddhism, Japanese Soto Zen, managed to do just that in the late nineteenth and early twentieth century, enthusiastically supporting the Imperial Japanese colonial expansion and the entry of Japan into the Second World War. That is the cost of flexibility; yet, equal or even greater harm can come from an insistence upon a rigid and literal interpretation of moral rules. Faced with these pluses and minuses, Buddhists are encouraged to be guided by the greater good principle, while not allowing themselves too much room to 'play fast and loose' with specific ethical guidelines, and above all to take personal responsibility for whatever they decide to do. This being so, it is not uncommon to find Buddhists who serve in the armed forces attending religious services beside those who are radical pacifists, each respecting the other and the honesty of their position.

Another interesting complication to the precept against taking life occurs when a person extends it to all life, not just human life. Many Buddhists feel an empathic bond to other animals, and, although that bond may be less intense than the one to their fellow humans, it nonetheless impels them to avoid the taking of animal life as well. Furthermore, some people also recognize in animals a form of struggle towards enlightenment which, although rudimentary, is nonetheless akin to our own; this provides added motivation to respect their lives. These points of view may find expression in such things as adhering to a vegetarian diet, working for animal welfare, personally adopting homeless animals as pets, using non-lethal methods of pest control, involvement in wildlife conservation projects, etcetera. For some individuals, this generalization of the reverence for life is taken even further, and they find that it leads them to a concern for the total environment of plants and animals alike, involving them in environmental issues on a local or global level. How far a person goes in this direction is again a matter of individual conscience, and devout Buddhists range in perspective all the way from those who refrain from gardening lest they inadvertently kill worms to those who find no problem with eating meat so long as the animal was not killed specifically for them. In another seeming paradox, sometimes those two positions are both held by the same person; the paradox resolves when one understands that the guiding principle for such a person is that of individual responsibility for the taking of animal life.

2. A second area for a Buddhist to consider on the topic of taking care with actions is how he or she relates to property. If someone is inwardly trying to give up attachments to things, it makes no sense for that person to be stealing things that don't belong to them. While this principle starts at the obvious level of criminal theft, it soon generalizes into more gray and uncomfortable areas, just like the previous one did. Where, for example, is the line between fair profit and exploitation? How many copies of a document, recorded television show, or computer program is it ethical to make and share without violating the spirit of copyright? When does taking time at work for the rest and refreshment that are helpful in doing a good job become cheating the employer out of the time for which we are paid? Here again, no formulas or easy answers are offered. It is a matter of individual responsibility for one's actions and of recognition that when mistakes are made there is no condemnation: just a need to learn from the mistake and to make the honest attempt to do better next time.

3. Another area of activity with which Buddhism suggests taking particular care is that of sexuality. Sexual ethics is always an uncomfortable topic for people to think about, yet those who wish to make an earnest effort to set aside their habits of delusion and attachment can hardly afford to ignore it. The very reasons why sexuality poses so many ethical difficulties for people—the

strength of our physical and emotional attachments in this area—are the reasons why Buddhism feels that it is so important to look clearly at what we are doing here, and to take care.

As a matter of fact, taking care, in the sense of deeply caring, is central to what sexuality is about. Even in the midst of a purely physical sexual relationship, people find that they cannot help but to start to care for the other person. It is from this natural caring, this natural love, that Buddhism bases its ethical principles in the sexual area. The more we are aware of the caring, and the less we complicate it with ideas, fantasies, and attachments, the more clear it is to see what is good to do. And 'what is good to do' is really quite simple: it is to conduct our sexual lives in such a way that love and caring are not cut off for anyone. Here too, empathy is central to the ethical process: if love and caring are the essence of sexuality for a person, how can that individual possibly participate in sexuality which denies love and caring to others? For this reason, Buddhists try not to engage in sexual activities that will harm themselves or others, that will betray the trust which people have placed in them, or that will use, abuse, or manipulate anyone. Exactly how that principle is applied is left up to the conscience of the individual in some schools of Buddhism, while in others there is an attempt to give specific guidelines suitable to the prevailing culture.

While a loving sexual relationship is central to the family life of many Buddhists, the ordained priests or monks of most schools of Buddhism are celibate. By the way, there is no difference between 'priests' and 'monks' in most Buddhist traditions; also, both terms can apply to either men or women in some schools, while other schools use 'monks and nuns' or terms that come from various Oriental languages. These celibate monastics choose to abstain from sexual activity altogether. In ancient times this was a requirement for ordination, and it still is in many types of Buddhism, although a married priesthood is common in the West, particularly in groups which come from some Japanese and Tibetan lineages.

Celibacy is a radical step, but, for monastics, it can serve several functions. It can encourage a deepening of their commitment to set aside all attachments, since sexuality is an area where so many of our most powerful desires and delusions seem to concentrate. Secondly, it can open a door to a degree of trust and intimacy with people which is often not found while the possibility of sexual involvement is present. And finally, by giving up the family life, priests are enabled to give all of their efforts to the service of their students and congregation.

The life of the celibate Buddhist monk is not for everyone, and celibacy is by no means a requirement for serious Buddhist practice; since Buddhism began, it has respected both the family life and that of the celibate monastic. For most people, the family is the center of their life, and taking care with sexuality helps the family to become the center of their religious practice as well. To develop a love which is not selfish and demanding is not easy, but it is possible. The very intensity of desires and illusions surrounding sexuality, which make it something to be given up by the monk, provide a fruitful field of practice for the householder. Facing the truth of one's attachments, fears, and fantasies in the sexual area is possible so long as one's actions are compassionate and ethical. Actually, the very struggle to face these and to hold to a standard of ethics in this area brings to light many useful insights. However, if a person abandons the principle of caring, then he or she is apt to become overwhelmed by the strength of their desires and lose perspective on what is real and what is merely the voice of passing attachment. One of the things which the voice of attachment is fond of telling people is "just one more time and you will have enough." This is typical of any addiction, and sexuality can easily turn into a powerful drug in the absence of the natural limits placed upon it by empathic caring.

4. Since the goal of this Path is the radical sobriety of enlightenment, it is hardly surprising that the normal sort of sobriety is among the things which are required. It would be next to impossible to achieve the goal of eliminating delusion while at the same time befuddling oneself with drink or drugs. In many traditional societies where the available intoxicants have been limited to alcohol and narcotics, this reason for abstinence is not difficult to understand, although it is plenty difficult to do if one happens to be an alcoholic or an addict. In such cultures, the only real question is how far to take the practice of sobriety. Some Buddhists practice total abstinence; traditionally that has been the position of most monks and some householders. Others see no harm in moderate use of alcohol, provided that a person does not drink to the point of intoxication and provided that there is no problem in stopping before that point. The use of narcotics is usually avoided completely, as their only purpose seems to be intoxication. I am not speaking, of course, about the medical use of narcotics, and this points to another area where personal discernment is required. Some medications have intoxicating side effects, and then a decision has to be made as to whether the medical benefits outweigh the costs of these side effects.

In some societies, including our own, things are more complicated because there is a class of drugs, the psychedelics, which are thought by some people to enhance rather than interfere with a person's ability to know spiritual truth. What attitude do Buddhists take towards these drugs? There is some debate on this point, but the majority of writers on Buddhist ethics oppose their use. There are basically two reasons for this. First, it is not at all certain that the experiences which these drugs produce are actually religious in nature. While there are some striking similarities between them and what some religious mystics have described, there are also significant differences. And the drugs are unpredictable: sometimes they produce religious-like experiences, sometimes they produce other experiences, some of which are quite harmful. Second, enlightenment is not simply an experience; it is an entire way of being which is inseparable from the whole of the Eightfold Path. So, even if a drug were able to reliably bring about religious experiences, it cannot set aside desire for us, it cannot behave ethically for us, and it cannot speak truthfully for us. Third, people who rely on a drug for their 'spiritual experiences' are actually telling themselves that they are inadequate: they are believing that they do not have the ability to find enlightenment with their own inner resources. One of the basic principles of Buddhism is that each of us is spiritually adequate and already has what we need in order to be spiritually complete.

The above four areas of right action, together with truthful and gentle speech, form the five ways of 'acting from enlightenment' which are agreed upon by almost all forms of Buddhism. They are the five basic ethical precepts by which most Buddhists live. Other precepts are added by various schools to round out and amplify these basic five. Most of these are implied by the five, by other aspects of the Eightfold Path, and/or by the general signs of enlightenment.

One of these additional precepts is to refrain from being proud of oneself and belittling others. Since pride is a sure sign of attachment, how could one willingly inflate it, much less seek to put down others? Another precept is not to hold back in giving either truth or wealth. Since charity is a sign of enlightened action, how could one practice stinginess in any form whatsoever? A third additional precept is to refrain from indulging anger. Since tenderness is another sign of enlightenment, and it is the wish of each person's heart to let it flow forth unboundedly, how could someone willingly hold onto and nourish angers and resentments which may arise, much less carry them to the point of actions which cause harm? A fourth is to refrain from defaming the Buddhist Way. Since this Way is a Buddhist's true refuge and its practice is enlightenment itself, how could a Buddhist be ungrateful for it, much less disparage it to others? Still other precepts offer guides to practicing respect and gratitude, to encouraging others in their practice, to using effort wisely within one's own practice, to caring for others who are ill or in need, and to not becoming caught up in distractions.

Aspect Five: Taking Care with Work

Work is another place where it is wise to take care, since work occupies a large part of our lives. Most forms of livelihood benefit the world and are suitable for a Buddhist. They may not be glamorous or seem all that benevolent while we are doing them; yet, in the big picture, it truly does matter that someone sweeps the streets, puts the right label on cans of peas, or keeps the world's financial currencies in balance. The benefit to others is obvious for those who work in the helping professions of medicine, teaching, counseling, raising a family, etcetera; nevertheless, Buddhism suggests that any job which assists humanity or the earth is worth doing and is worthy of respect. Undertaking any of these careers is what is known as the Path aspect of 'right livelihood.'

There are a few ways of earning a living, however, which are of doubtful merit: they either involve things which seem to do harm or which appear to be utterly useless. Most of the former can be identified by looking at them in terms of right speech and right action. For example, a few forms of political work, public relations, and the like seem to require of people that they actually deceive others. It is not easy to see how someone could hold such a job without chronically lying. There are other careers which require killing as part of the job: professional hunting or fishing, working in a slaughter house, or being involved in administering capital punishment would be examples. Most Buddhists would find these types of work to violate their conscience. The principle of violating a precept in order to promote a greater good or inhibit a greater harm can be applied to the killing which may occur as part of military and police work, but does the same principle apply to the jobs that I just mentioned? Does it apply to the making or sale of armaments? And, if it does apply, where does a person draw the line: are there some weapons which are so awful that a person of conscience simply cannot be involved in making them, for instance?

If, for a particular individual, the 'greater good principle' does not justify doing an activity, then how much distance does that person need to keep from it? For example, to return to the question of making arms, is it ethical to make components, some of which are then used in the making of weapons; to make computer programs that are used to make the components; to invest money in the companies which make the programs, etcetera? To take a different example, is it ethical to work in a laboratory which produces wonderful medicines to help people but does so at the cost of creating suffering and death for thousands of laboratory animals? These kinds of decisions are brought into focus for a Buddhist by the Path aspect of right livelihood, with the understanding that there are no easy answers and that people will take personal responsibility for their actions.

Similar hard choices arise when the Buddhist considers the ethical principle of refraining from theft: things get subtle once he or she looks past the obviously unwise livelihoods of being a burglar or a swindler. To be a farmer, for instance, is clearly a right livelihood which benefits people by feeding them; but what if the farming is done in a way which depletes the soil? Is that stealing from future generations in order to feed this one? Do the benefits outweigh the costs, or not? To be a forester who both cares for the land and provides wood for housing is most excellent, but if that forester's company starts cutting more trees than they plant, is this still right livelihood?

Most Buddhists would feel that people who work as prostitutes or pornography producers coarsen themselves and place obstacles in the way of both their own Buddhist spiritual development and that of others. But what about creating advertising which plays upon people's sexual fantasies in order to sell products?

Or, is it ethical for a Buddhist to be involved in making movies which make a useful social point yet rely upon stimulating people's sexual desires in order to get them to the box office?

As for the area of drink and drugs, examples of work which most Buddhists would avoid would include those of making or selling liquor or illegal drugs. This seems to be a pretty easily defined area where right and wrong livelihoods can be clearly identified, yet gray areas are not far off here, as well. Consider the farmer again: is it ethical for him or her to sell grain to a distillery? Suppose that a doctor has a patient on chemotherapy for cancer, a patient who could benefit from using marijuana to overcome some of the side effects of the cancer medications; is it wise to recommend this drug to the patient or not? And then there are the drugs of ideology and false idealism. If a person is employed in government, is it all right to knowingly 'push' these onto people in order to get them to support a worthwhile social action? It is not always easy to tell whether a particular way of work might be doing more harm than good.

The other question which comes up when thinking about right livelihood is whether a person's work does any good at all. Even if a job does no harm, if it is utterly useless is it really a wise way to spend one's days? Answering this question is perhaps even more a matter of individual conscience than answering the previous one. How do you decide if something is useful or not? Yet this is a question which many people, Buddhists and non-Buddhists alike, find themselves asking about their work as they enter middle age. In those moments of quiet reflection, this seems to matter; so it may be well to ask it from time to time, before we find ourselves having spent all of our working life doing something that we regret because of its meaninglessness. A job does not have to be highly paid or glamorous in order to be meaningful; as a matter of fact, some very useful careers are of low social status. So, the questions which Buddhists tend to ask themselves are whether or not someone benefits, whether or not the world is a little bit better for them having gone to work that day, or what the world would be like if no one did their job.

These are some of the difficult questions about work which the Path invites Buddhists to ask of themselves. There are often no easy or simple answers. Yet the questions are worth asking, as at the end of the day (and at the end of one's life) these things make a difference. It is not that most Buddhists spend a lot of time thinking about these things as abstract issues; however, when a particular concern of this type arises, it seems better to face it immediately, and take responsibility for answering it, than to look the other way and risk undertaking a livelihood which will be a source of deep regrets later.

Aspect Six: Making Wise Effort

This step, and the two to follow, return our attention to the 'inner work' of doing something about how we *are* instead of about what we *do*. And, at this point it becomes more clear how all of the parts of the Eightfold Path work together, each support-ing and extending the others. It is pretty obvious that none of the other Path aspects will mean much to a person unless there is a willingness to put some effort into making changes in how life is lived. 'Right effort,' as this step is called, can be as simple as tak-ing all of the other Path aspects seriously and trying to put them into effect. In the beginning many Buddhists view right effort in this way; undoubtedly this view is needed, and it will take a per-son quite a long ways towards enlightenment.

But at some point a paradox arises. It is clear enough that unless a person tries to make some changes, there is no point in continuing with Buddhist training. The trouble comes when someone realizes that letting go of 'trying' is itself one of the changes that needs to be made! 'Trying' creates a sort of separa-tion between ourselves and what we do: there is the doing and then there is a self that is trying. After a while that separation starts to get in the way, since one of the essential things about enlightenment is that it is one and undivided. What can be done about this?

Some Buddhist teachings talk about 'effortless effort' or the 'goal of goalessness,' and sometimes this sounds as if the religion is saying that all we need to do is 'do what comes naturally.' And in a sense that is true. But what is needed is not doing what comes naturally to our selfish mind, for to do this would be simply to indulge impulsiveness, to go back to faster horses, wilder lovers, and more whiskey. Instead, Buddhists must find a way to do what comes naturally to something else within themselves. This 'something else' is what some schools of Buddhism call 'Buddha Nature' or 'the Mind that seeks the Way'. It is that within ourselves which has always been attuned to the truth, and it has already been mentioned in the section about right thought. Other forms of Buddhism refer to that which guides a person as 'insight,' the inner wisdom which is developed over time and training in the Path. Still others view it as a transcendental being and give It a name such as 'Prajnaparamita,' 'Manjusri Bodhisattva,' or 'Amida Buddha.' Whatever it may be called and however it may be viewed, finding it is one of the things which Buddhist training is all about. When a person discovers the existence of this 'something else,' the paradox of right effort can be solved, because it becomes apparent that there is more than one sort of effort.

The one which we are used to is the effort in which we are in control: I have a goal or ideal and direct my behavior in ways which I think will achieve it. This is the sort of effort which starts to cause difficulties over the course of Buddhist training. The problem with ideals has already been mentioned; an even more fundamental problem will be gone into later in the book—there is a real question as to whether or not 'I' even exist in the first place. Furthermore, just as ideals may be nice thoughts but are lousy descriptions of how the world really works, the same applies to our ideas about how to achieve the changes we desire. Whatever 'we' may be, we don't seem to be wise enough to direct or control our lives in the long run: our best laid plans never seem to get us where we thought they would. With all of these difficulties, it is small wonder that this type of effort at reforming ourselves often goes awry.

However, there is another type of effort entirely, an effort which arises from the 'something else.' It is more a matter of willingness than of will. It is the willingness to let go of things moment-by-moment: ideas, opinions, wants, fears, ideals, judgments,…*everything*. It is the willingness at all times to learn, to be open to seeing in new ways. And it is the willingness to do whatever comes next. 'Doing what comes next' seems to come from honesty and courage rather than from will. The honesty is that of looking straight at what lies before us, at what is shown to us simply and clearly by the 'something else.' And this, in turn, involves trust: trust that wisdom and compassion really do exist somewhere within ourselves, trust that they can do their work without us having to control or direct anything, and trust that we can perceive their teachings directly from the experience of our senses without analyzing, fearing, judging, doubting, or worrying about what we discern. The courage involved in this type of effort is the courage to do what is obviously to be done and to abstain from what is obviously to be abstained from. This, then, is the 'effortless effort.' No 'me' is involved, no ideals, no thinking or planning, no control, no direction. The work is that of the 'something else'; the direction appears naturally when we stop chattering to ourselves and let the 'something else' get a word in edgewise; the trust is placed in the wisdom of the 'something else.' For each individual, there are just things which are clearly to be done and things which are clearly not to be done: it's that simple.

Since we are all human and likely to remain so, we have blind spots which get in the way of this process. For instance, our hidden wants and fears can get in the way of seeing clearly the simple fact of what comes next. We are also quite capable of mistaking our own desires for the wisdom of 'something else.' Recognizing this,

Buddhism provides guidelines to make it safe to actually exercise the courage to do what must be done. Among these are the various precepts which have been mentioned in the previous three sections. The source of all of these precepts is the same 'something else' which we are trusting to make clear to us what is to be done. So, if we are seeing clearly, what we are shown cannot be in conflict with these precepts. In this way, the aspect of right effort gives the strength and courage to follow right speech, right action, and right livelihood, and those three aspects make it safe to engage without compromise in right effort.

In addition to the precepts, there are other checks and balances which make it safe for a follower of Buddhism to develop and trust his or her own spiritual intuition about the 'something else.' Chief among these is what is known as the 'Three Refuges' or 'Three Treasures.' In all matters of importance, the Buddhist religion calls upon its adherents to seek guidance from all three of these refuges simultaneously. The first of them is the Buddha, and in some schools this includes the personal spiritual intuition and discernment, which are regarded as a form of 'inner Buddha Nature.' However, even in these schools, the Buddha Refuge includes a lot more than this: it also involves respecting the enlightened nature of all people, following the example of the historical founder of Buddhism, and acknowledging a Truth within the universe that is far greater than oneself. At the same time that the individual seeks guidance from the Buddha Refuge, he or she also turns for advice to the totality of the Buddhist teachings, called the 'Dharma,' and to the community of Buddhist teachers and fellow students alive today, called the 'Sangha.' These three interlocking refuges, together with the precepts, act as a safe framework within which one's own discernment and spiritual intuition may be viewed. Since Buddhism regards truth as being one and undivided, it holds that there cannot be real conflicts between a Buddhist's own inner wisdom and either the precepts or the Triple Refuge.

This means that any *apparent* conflicts between these things, when they arise, cannot be what they seem. And, generally, such apparent conflicts indicate that there is a 'piece of the puzzle' which has yet to be seen. So, when these conflicts do appear, it is recommended that a Buddhist wait and take more refuge before acting, in the faith that things will become clear. For example, when what a person discerns is in conflict with what another trusted Sangha member perceives, the individual tries to avoid assuming that one of them must be right, the other wrong. Occasionally, of course, that may be true (each being human and having blind spots), but time and training will make this clear; arguing about it, whether inside an individual's own head or with the other person, is not the best way to clarify it. More likely, however, it is not a matter of right and wrong: it is a case of what I call the 'pussycat problem.' One person sees a whisker, and it is actually there; the other sees an ear, and it is there, too. Argument as to whether it is really a whisker or an ear is not what is needed. Instead, further refuge taking and ongoing training in the Eightfold Path reveal a paw and a nose; it becomes apparent that what they were dealing with was something larger than just an ear or just a whisker: it was a pussycat. In a way, both were right and both were wrong. Of course, it might also be a skunk. So there might be some wisdom in waiting and training just a bit longer, until a tail appears, before a person reaches out and starts stroking that ear. Skunks are just as nice as pussycats, but they don't take kindly to being touched: a different approach is called for! Then again, there are times when we cannot wait to act: we have to take up our courage, do the best we can, and be willing to take the consequences. All of this is part of right effort.

Putting this type of effort into practice requires a tolerance for not knowing things. Even when the next step is discerned in a simple and clear way, it isn't really *known*. Perhaps it is seen, heard, felt, or intuitively sensed; but it is not *known* in the way one's mind would like. This 'not knowing' seems to be characteristic of

Buddhist training: the farther people get into it, the less they seem to 'know,' even as there is greater certainty about the simple things which appear right in front of them. This type of 'not knowing' is actually an aspect of wisdom, and strange as it may seem, it is far more useful than the knowing which we tend to want. In fact, it is usually 'knowing' which causes problems in the practice of right effort. When people 'know' how they should be living their lives, they are apt to judge themselves by that standard and try to use will power to force themselves to measure up. The standard, the judging, the forcing, and the measuring are all subtle forms of attachment or delusion, and so they inevitably lead to more suffering instead of to liberation. If, however, a person can simply go onward in honest unknowing, all of that is avoided.

Why, then, does an Eightfold Path exist? Isn't its purpose to make known to Buddhists how to live and train effectively? At one level of meaning, of course it is; and at another level, that is not its purpose at all. It is not a list of things to be known and done, not a standard by which Buddhists are expected to measure themselves or others, not a set of tools with which to fix oneself. It is, instead, more like a *doorway*. It is to be walked through daily, with honesty and courage, in unknowing. Its true place is in the innermost heart, not in the knowing mind. It does its work by posing honest questions and by pointing to the simple next step. The Buddhist's task is to ask those questions and to take that step, as best he or she can, at each moment. That is all that Buddhism ever requires.

Aspect Seven: Mindfulness

If the Buddhist is asked to give up knowing in the usual sense, and to trust in the wisdom of 'something else,' it would be really helpful if there was a way of developing that kind of wisdom. Actually, there are two ways of doing this, and they form the final two aspects of the Path. They are somewhat related, yet different enough and important enough to each be given their own separate place.

The first of these is mindfulness. The essential ingredients of this practice are to pay very close attention to what one is doing, to be fully aware of it, and when one's attention wanders off to something else, to bring it back again. In the practice of mindfulness, attention and awareness are applied without inner reactions to the things one is aware of. It is a neutral sort of observation of oneself and the world, uncomplicated by thoughts, feelings, judgments, and the like. The heart of this type of practice, in other words, is simply to be fully aware of what exists, with nothing added and nothing hidden from view. This way of training is bound to assist a Buddhist with what he or she is trying to do: just to be aware of things, large and small, on a daily basis cannot help but lay the groundwork for being able to view the entire universe for what it really is. Mindfulness is a type of truthfulness; it is the truthful perception of exactly what is really there.

Different schools of Buddhism have various ways of doing this practice, and these ways involve directing the attention to many different things. Some traditions have a carefully prescribed program of first directing the mind to be fully aware of simple things and then systematically turning that mindful attention to more and more subtle aspects of reality. Others teach their followers one unified practice which they can apply to everything in life.

It is a bit hard to describe the practice of mindfulness in the abstract; so, to give a flavor of what it is like, I will explain how to do one of the latter types, which is the way of my own tradition, Soto Zen Buddhism. The method is incredibly simple and requires nothing more than the willingness to keep doing it with some persistence. Because of this, and because its application is so general, it has been used not only by Buddhists but also by non-Buddhists to deepen their religious insight. It can be summarized in five steps:

1. Do one thing at a time.
2. Pay full attention to what you are doing.
3. When your mind wanders to something else, bring it back.

4. Repeat step number three a few hundred thousand times.

5. And, if your mind keeps wandering to the same thing over and over, stop for a minute and pay attention to the distraction: maybe it is trying to tell you something.

The reason for the first two steps is that, if we accept the principle that truth is one and undivided, then it can only be realized by a mind which is itself unified. A unified mind requires that one's attention be full and focused, not scattered and divided. Mindfulness is the practice of doing just that. For example, people who wish to engage in this type of mindfulness practice might forgo their habit of eating breakfast, talking to their spouse, and watching the morning news all at the same time. Planning your ten o'clock meeting while you drive to work is out; so is thinking about your vacation while you wash the dishes, worrying about your finances while you plant the garden, and even reading a magazine while you're on the toilet. This is quite easy to do, but one of the problems is that, for most people, there are many things which they could (or worse yet, should) be doing at any given time, and the temptation to do more than one is great. A person in this situation might find it helpful to add a 'step zero' before the first of the five steps. Step zero is to decide what is the single most important thing to be doing at this moment. Then, do it.

Mindfulness practice requires that we not only do one thing at a time, but also that we pay full attention to what we are doing. However, the sort of attention that is paid is not quite what one might expect. While it is focused, it is also wide-ranging and fluid. One does not exclude anything from mind: thoughts, perceptions, emotions, intuitions, etcetera. Yet whenever you become aware of having gotten caught in, or engaged by, any of these things, you bring your mind back to focus on the activity at hand. It is very important to understand this step. Mindfulness training is not a rigid focusing of the concentration upon one object to the exclusion of all other things. That would be to create a duality, to divide up the world. It would also be dangerous: people who exclude things from awareness tend to have accidents. There is a place for concentration (though not of a dualistic sort) in the next Path aspect, meditation. Here, in the practice of mindfulness, you exclude nothing from awareness. And when you realize that you have become distracted, then you return your attention gently to the present activity.

Step four acknowledges that this 'returning to the present' may have to be repeated hundreds, perhaps thousands, of times a day. In the beginning it is quite normal for the mind to wander off again almost immediately, and there is a certain amount of trial and error involved in learning how to bring back the attention with gentleness and patience.

The first four steps are pretty straightforward; step five, however, requires more explanation. Occasionally a thought, feeling, etcetera, will just not leave you alone. No matter how many times you bring your mind back to the activity at hand, this particular thought keeps insisting itself upon your mind. Sometimes this is simply a particularly pesky distraction, but at other times there is a good reason for this: the thought or feeling is trying to tell you something. For this reason, it is wise to stop what you are doing and take that 'distraction' seriously for a moment. In other words, make thinking about that topic the 'one thing you are doing now.' When such a 'distraction' isn't really a distraction, its most common causes are: that there is something else which is more urgent than what you are doing, that there is something that you have left unfinished or wrong or dangerous, or that there is a nice ripe insight waiting to come into your awareness if given the chance. If none of these things seem to be happening, and there does not appear to be anything further to be learned from examining the nagging thought, then that thought may well be simply a distraction after all: an old habit of mind that is hard to change. And the thing to do is to go back to what you were doing before, and once again give it your full attention.

If a 'distraction' is actually telling a person something important, then this often means that it is necessary to put aside the first activity and start doing the more important thing. This switch of attention can also become necessary when it is just obvious at some point that something else needs to be done. The ability to switch attention from one activity to another, readily and without attachment, does not come easily for most of us. But, with practice, it can be cultivated, and it is an important aspect of mindfulness. This aspect of the Eightfold Path is like driving a car on an icy road: keep a gentle hand on the wheel, keep your eyes on the road (but don't ignore your peripheral vision), and when you see another car skidding towards you, change course smoothly and don't insist on the right of way!

Mindfulness practice is easy to describe and simple to do. Yet, as with any spiritual practice, it has its difficulties. One is the fear that "I'll never get my work done if I only do one thing at a time." This is a reasonable concern; fortunately however, it is unfounded. What actually happens for most people, after the first few days of awkwardness, is that mindfulness enables them to do more and better work. This may be because the advantage in time saved when one does several things at once is more than offset by the increased efficiency and decreased tension that results from the mindful approach.

A second problem is that practicing mindfulness is a lot of work. This is true enough, particularly in the beginning. After a while, the whole thing becomes almost second nature, but initially a person has to keep coming back to it again and again, even when it seems that no progress is being made. This is where faith, trust, and right effort come in. One of the characteristics of Buddhism as a religion is that it invites people to actually do things differently on a day-to-day basis, and this is undoubtedly work. It also takes time for this practice, and the other aspects of the Eightfold Path, to have their effects. But then, nobody promised that radical sobriety would come quickly and easily.

Finally, engaging in mindfulness practice can interfere with people's usual social interactions. This is true, and because of this a person may not wish to do it all the time. Even in Buddhist monasteries a certain rest from this practice is built into the schedule, and the monks sometimes enjoy social conversation while drinking tea or eating an informal meal. These breaks also keep the trainee from inadvertently doing the practice so intensely that it becomes something grim and unpleasant. In this, as in all things, Buddhism urges a middle way between self-indulgence and austerity. So, if you are practicing mindfulness, sometimes you may want to eat breakfast and talk to your spouse at the same time, after all. Doing this from time to time is not a problem: enjoy the meal together (and you will probably enjoy it more if you aren't also watching television).

In sum, the method of doing this form of mindfulness training is to do one thing at a time—and pay attention to it—as much as it seems wise to do so, to bring your mind back gently each time it wanders, but not to be so strict with yourself that you make the practice unpalatable. Done in this way, the exercise of mindfulness is refreshing, liberating, and energizing. And, whatever form of mindfulness practice an individual may undertake, it acts to deepen insight, increase awareness, promote all acceptance, and reduce attachment. It also tends towards right understanding and makes the reasons for practicing right action, speech, and livelihood more obvious. It undermines distraction and weakens the power of many of the intoxicants of daily life. No wonder it is an important part of the Eightfold Path.

Aspect Eight: Meditation

Meditation is the most profound and mysterious aspect of the Path. Exactly what meditation is, what it does, and how it acts, are not fully known. Yet there is no doubt that the practice of meditation is of great importance in living the Buddhist life. It is sort of like the locomotive that powers the train of the Eightfold

Path: with it, all the rest goes forward; without it, nothing moves much, unless perhaps to roll backwards down hill.

Different schools of Buddhism practice meditation of varying types; however, most of these types have this in common: concentration (or one-pointedness of mind) and awareness (or insight into things-as-they-are). In some types of Buddhist meditation, concentration and awareness are taught and practiced separately; others combine them together. Some traditions teach a graduated sequence of meditations; others teach one general form of meditation which they recommend throughout the course of a person's entire life. Unlike mindfulness, which is easily described and can be put into practice without personal instruction, most forms of meditation need to be learned personally from a qualified instructor. For this reason, I will not attempt to give a detailed description of how meditation is done, even as an example. Instead, I will attempt to say just enough about it to give a flavor of what it is about.

While mindfulness can be practiced anywhere at any time, meditation is a more formal practice which generally requires a person to stop other activities and set aside a time and a place for meditation and for nothing else. This is one reason why many Buddhists have a space in their home that they reserve for meditation. This space is kept as a place of quiet refuge from daily life. It is kept particularly clean and fresh, with flowers and incense often being provided. There may be a small family altar, sometimes with an image of a Buddha upon it, seated in the classic meditation posture. This is the most common posture seen in such statues: cross-legged, with back erect, head balanced, eyes cast down gently, and hands one atop the other in the lap.

This is not the only posture in which meditation can be done, however. Depending upon which type of Buddhism people follow and upon the abilities of the body, some people meditate in postures with one leg on top of (or in front of) the other, kneeling, sitting on a chair, or even lying down, if need be. While there are many possible postures, the position of the body is important, and not any old posture will do. Balance, harmony, centeredness, ease, and alertness are important physical aspects of the practice. The posture also needs to be one which a person can hold for a while, usually somewhere around a half-hour to forty-five minutes depending upon the type of meditation, without becoming tense, sore, or sleepy.

The mental aspect of meditation is more difficult to describe than the physical one, and it also varies considerably across different schools of Buddhism. As with mindfulness, there is an element of paying close attention, but in some forms of meditation this is taken further and becomes actual concentration or one-pointedness of mind. Having already simplified his or her situation by sitting still in a quiet place, the meditator turns the attention to one simple thing. Sometimes this may be a body process such as the breath coming in and out of the nostrils, or the abdomen rising and falling with breathing. In other forms of meditation one might concentrate upon visualizations of colors, forms, or images, upon sacred sounds (called 'mantras'), body positions (called 'mudras'), or brief passages of ancient texts which challenge one to drop off conceptual thinking (called 'koans'). Other forms of Buddhist meditation use a more general focus. For instance, the one which is practiced by my own Soto Zen tradition involves paying close attention to the fact of simply sitting there. That is the only meditation subject we use, and we use it for beginners and experts alike.

Whatever the focus may be, the concentration element in meditation needs to be done in a way which allows the mind to become quiet and centered, and which neither dulls the mind into blankness nor divides the person into 'observer' and 'observed.' It requires patient trial and error to find a way to actually do that, and this is one of the areas in which expert advice is very helpful.

In addition to the element of concentration, many forms of Buddhist meditation also contain an element of insight, of heightened awareness of 'things as they are.' Again, there are many ways of doing this, but what they have in common is that the meditator is asked to bring his or her mind back to the meditation subject whenever it wanders off. And wander it will! Anyone who tries to do meditation will notice that maintaining an alert, focused, aware mind that is not tense and yet is fully attentive to the meditation subject is not easy.

All of one's habits of mind run contrary to this. We want distraction, entertainment, or excitement; we think that we need to worry, plan, or fear; or we simply babble endlessly to ourselves. These are habits of intoxication: they are the ways in which we maintain both our attachments and our addictions, and meditation cuts at the roots of all of them. The simple fact of not allowing one's mind to run off in these directions for awhile, done time and again over the years, causes quite remarkable things to happen. The strength of the attachments decreases, the chatter drops away, and simple obvious insight into 'things as they are' arises in their place.

As with the results of other aspects of the Path, this all takes time and cannot be forced nor directed by the will. The meditator does not, for instance, try to actively stop the distractions from arising nor blank out the mind to the point where there is no awareness at all. These approaches would seriously unbalance the harmony of meditation: the first one by increasing concentration to the point of excluding awareness, the second by decreasing awareness to the point that only concentration is left. On the other hand, to willingly 'leave one's sitting place' and allow one's mind to be captured and carried away by a particular thought or feeling, thus turning what was simply a passing thought into a ten minute chain of thinking, is not done either. Here, the concentration has been insufficient, and awareness has lost touch entirely with the meditation subject. Whenever this happens, depending upon the type of meditation, the person either simply becomes aware of the distraction and mentally notes it (for example, "worrying, worrying" or "babbling, babbling"), or they just gently bring their attention back to the breathing, the mantra, the visualization, to just sitting, etcetera. How to do this is another area that seems to require a fair amount of trial and error learning, and ongoing consultation with an experienced teacher of meditation is advisable.

Occasionally, interesting and exciting things happen during meditation; various types of spiritual experiences sometimes occur. But that is not the way it is for everyone, and even for those to whom interesting things happen, most of the time nothing much seems to 'happen' at all. With experience and a good teacher, the meditator learns to take all of this in stride, learning from, but not being attached to, the former, and not becoming discouraged by the latter. The Path aspect of meditation is not done in order to have spiritual experiences, nor does the lack of them imply that anything is wrong. Meditation cannot be easily judged or measured—which is probably just as well, since measuring and judging are precisely some of the things which right thought teaches us to set aside. As a matter of fact, when people are meditating they don't even know that they are doing it. That sounds strange, but the reason is actually very simple: if a person were to know that he or she was doing it, then part of the person would be doing it and another part would be knowing that it's being done. This would create a division in a mind that, by its very essence, is one and undivided. So, if a person knows that they are meditating, it's a pretty good sign that they aren't! But you can know that you are not meditating, and that is all one needs to know, because that is the only time when something needs to be done differently. When you are aware of being distracted, then you have the opportunity to bring your attention back to the meditation subject.

Meditation is impossible to fully understand or assess with the thinking mind; its work is done in ways that are not obvious. Ask experienced meditators why they do it and you often won't get very logical answers. But they keep doing it, and so have the great

Buddhist teachers throughout time. Even after full enlightenment they don't stop; especially after full enlightenment they don't stop. Whatever meditation may be, it is central to the Buddhist life of radical sobriety.

4.
Things Are Not
What They Seem

The Four Noble Truths, the Law of Change, and the Eightfold Path are the foundations of Buddhism. When people put these principles into practice, their view of the world begins to change. This change is gradual and subtle, yet also far-reaching. The practice of Buddhism leads people to some surprising conclusions and a rather unique perspective on things. A book like this can only describe such a viewpoint in words; those who actually live by the Buddhist Way experience it directly and personally.

About Things

The Law of Change, for example, has some startling implications when it is actually taken as the basis of a person's way of seeing the world. We usually regard material objects—things—as being separate and independent from one another and from us. However, if everything is always changing, what is a 'thing,' really? In the first chapter I used this book as an example and mentioned how it was never quite the same from moment to moment. If it is different now than it was a minute ago, which one is the real book? You could say that they both are. But notice that, even though we may *say* that they are 'the same thing,' they actually aren't the same. So, what does it really mean to say that they are 'the same thing'? And suppose you get fed up with my ramblings and decide to burn this book in the fireplace. When, exactly, does it stop being 'a book'? And what about those chemicals that you sniffed up when you smelled the book a few chapters ago, are they still 'the book' or are they now 'you'?

Interesting questions. In one sense these questions aren't really about books and fireplaces and you: they're about how we view the world and what we tell ourselves about it. We tell ourselves that there are 'things' out there, but that is actually a handy little fiction. There really is no such thing as 'this book'; there is only an ever-changing flow of space/time/being which we sometimes find useful to divide up in our minds and call one of the parts that we have mentally created 'a book.' After a while, a Buddhist actually starts to see the universe this way.

Now don't get me wrong, it is not that Buddhists become unable to perceive books as separate sorts of 'things.' In fact, they'd have a very hard time getting through life if they couldn't make use of the usual sorts of little fictions. It is very useful, for example, to call a large metallic perception 'a bus' and to tell myself that 'it' is coming down 'the road' that 'I' am walking across: better get out of the way! Children spend the first few years of their lives learning how to create exactly these sorts of handy fictions, and so they pull themselves away from relating to the world as simply a swirl of change and flow. People who can't learn to do that (and there are some) have a real tough time in this world! Buddhism is a practical religion: it doesn't teach that to live by truth requires us to walk out in front of buses. Instead, it leads people gradually into seeing our little fictions for what they are and simultaneously to recognizing a whole other level of reality. One can continue to make use of the handy fiction that 'things exist' while at the same time not entirely believing that the world is populated with 'things' that 'act' on 'each other.' This enables a person to live normally and still have room in the mind to experience the reality of the undivided, ever-changing flow of space/time/being.

Words and thoughts are at the core of this system of little fictions, but Buddhism continues to use them anyway. This is because if people didn't use them, there would be no way to communicate about this stuff with each other: we'd all be reduced to pointing and grunting. So, using words, the ancient Buddhist texts point out that truth itself is not to be found in words, and then they go right on using words to teach about it! That is another reason why many of the classic Buddhist writings can seem a bit strange and paradoxical. They weren't trying to be mysterious; they were trying to be as clear and straightforward as possible in exploring truth. It is just that human nature requires that if we are going to talk about a truth that exists beyond words and thoughts, we have to use words and thoughts to do it.

And that's what I'll have to continue to do here; because this is a book, and books are made of words. I can't step out of the book and point and grunt at you. Or shout, or hit you with a stick, or tug at your sleeve, or point at the moon—which ancient Buddhist teachers, particularly in the Zen schools, have sometimes done. As with the apparently paradoxical words of Buddhist writings, so it is with the strange antics you sometimes read about Buddhist teachers. They didn't do such things because they were trying to be cute or mystifying; they were practical women and men who were trying to point out to their students, as simply and clearly as they could, that there is a truth deeper than the little fictions of 'words' and 'things.' By the way, since you now know that I don't believe that 'words' really exist but I'm going to use them anyway, I can stop putting all sorts of words in quotation marks as a way of telling you that I don't quite believe them. Otherwise 'I'll' 'soon' 'have' 'to' 'start' 'putting' 'them' 'all' 'in' 'quotation' 'marks'— and then you really will want to throw this book into the fire!

About The Universe

So, if words and things are simply handy fictions, does the flow of space/time/being have *any* properties that are true and reliable? Buddhism holds that it does. Actually, the first one has already been hinted at. If things don't really exist as such, then a true property of the universe is that it is empty of all things, and all things are fundamentally empty. Now, when Buddhists talk about emptiness in this way they don't mean that there is nothing there: that it's all just a big, fat zero. Some philosophers have believed in that sort of ultimate nothingness (they're usually a pretty gloomy bunch in consequence), but that's not the kind of emptiness Buddhists are talking about. Instead of seeing the world as a place where there's *nothing*, they see it as a place where there is *no thing*. When an individual can set aside the useful fictions of thoughts, words and things, he or she can actually see/understand/be this emptiness of the universe. From that perspective one can simultaneously see the unreality of the bus, stand in awe of the wonder of the flow of space/time/being, and still cross roads without getting squished.

I say 'the wonder' of the flow of the universe because there is yet another consequence of the Law of Change. The first is that everything is always changing; the second is that it's empty; and the third is hard to describe: the ancient scriptures mention that a property of the flow is that it is unborn, unbecome, unmade, and unconditioned. Because it is unborn it is also undying and eternal; because it is unbecome and unmade it is void of all that can be known and grasped and therefore pure and tranquil; because it is unconditioned by other causes it is complete as it is, and it is a true refuge. In other words, this universe of ours is not only changing and empty but also at the very same time it is utterly chock-full and awesome. Another way to put this is that *space/time/being itself is ultimate truth, and to be at one with it is to find the peace we all are searching for.* To live uncompromisingly by the Law of Change leads to the same enlightened end-point that is described by the Four Noble Truths and reached through living the Eightfold Path. All of the basic aspects of Buddhism apparently lead to this same end-point.

Because we are human and we want to give this end-point a name, we call it 'nirvana,' but that doesn't make it a thing, an experience, a state of mind, or any-thing else. And it is not some special place, like the heaven of most other religions: it is precisely this world—the very world which is usually the cause of our unhappiness and dissatisfaction—seen for what it truly is. Because descriptions of nirvana are sometimes so attractive, Buddhists have to take care lest it become the 'fastest horse of all,' something to be grabbed at, which simply causes more frustration. It helps to remember that 'nirvana' is just another word, another convenient fiction, which we use to describe something beyond thoughts and words.

If 'nirvana' is the word used to describe the ultimate in Buddhism, then what does 'enlightenment' refer to? Well, sometimes they mean the same thing; they are more or less interchangeable. But while 'nirvana' always refers to the ultimate end-point, 'enlightenment' can also be used to describe a person's state of being at *any* moment in which they are fully one with the flow of space/time/being, even if in the next moment they grab onto something and return to their old way of viewing things. That is not the same as nirvana, because it is temporary. Yet it is not completely different, either. Even one moment in which all cravings are absent provides a profound experience of peace; even one instant of unhindered oneness with the flow of space/time/being gives an insight into the true nature of ourselves and the world. And the absence of craving, or the presence of oneness, doesn't even have to be complete in order for wonderful things to happen.

Even a moment of getting close to these conditions allows for a taste, a deep drink, of enlightenment, which is enough to change a person's life. And that is a good thing, because going deeply and thoroughly into all of Buddhist training requires making massive changes in one's entire way of being: it is a lifetime's work. The fact that lesser changes, and temporary moments of success along the way, have deeply beneficial and lasting consequences is what keeps most Buddhists going. Buddhism is not an 'either-or' sort of religion: a person is not either lost or saved, not either bound for hell or for heaven. In Buddhism one evolves, or grows, out from ignorance and into truth. Each step along the way, whether large or small, whether recognized by the person or unrecognized, has its effects. Every time we let go of grasping after things, even if we only manage to do it for a moment, we increase our tranquillity and clarify our understanding of truth. Since this is so, the very process of following the Eightfold Path of Buddhist training is enlightenment manifesting itself in the world. This is the reason why some ancient Buddhist works have gone so far as to say that *training itself is enlightenment, and enlightenment is the process of training.* So, which is the end-point and which is the process? The end becomes the means and the means becomes the end—and both merge into one flow of space/time/being.

What About You and Me?

Well, what about us? If things are actually convenient little fictions, is the same true of us? If we are somehow different from things and are more than just convenient names given to momentary positions in the universal flow, then we'd better actually exist somewhere, as separate and independent selves which are somehow constant throughout our lives. Where might this separate and constant self exist?

It can't be in our bodies, since they change subtly day to day, and change in big ways over longer periods of time. At the age of fifty-six, I am definitely aware that my body is not the same as when I was twenty! And, so I am told, after a few years most of the cells that make up my body today will be gone, replaced by others which are similar in function but not exactly the same. Even if I were to suffer a terrible accident and lose an arm, I would still regard myself as 'me.' I'd say, "It's still me, but without an arm."

The self can't really reside in our minds, either. Leaving aside the question of whether or not there is such a thing as a mind separate from the nerve cells that make up the brain, it too is always changing. Actually, if we pay close attention, we can see that it changes even more rapidly than the body. No two thought-moments are exactly the same. My mental experience of typing the previous sentence has now passed, and I can never get it back. I can remember it (sort of), but that is by no means the same as being there again. If my self is my mind, then I am certainly not the comfortable, constant sort of a thing that calling me 'me' implies.

Might the self be found within consciousness? Or perhaps the continuity of consciousness? Well, there does seem to be something constant and uninterrupted about my consciousness. That is, until I go to sleep. Do I cease to exist when I am asleep? In order to go to sleep I do have to let go of a lot of things, including consciousness itself. And the experience of being me is clearly gone while I am asleep. To think of the self as continuity of consciousness works pretty well until we realize that it means that we'd have to say that the self ceases to exist each evening and a new one is born the following morning. That isn't even close to what we would want to call 'me.' To get around that problem, I might sort of vaguely assume that, because the consciousness of today includes a memory of yesterday, my self must have gone somewhere while I was asleep and returned in the morning. But that actually doesn't solve the problem, either. Where did I go?

Mostly, we solve this problem by not inquiring too carefully into it. And that works fine for most purposes. Having the idea that each of us exists as a comfortably constant sort of a self, separate from each other and the world, and able to act upon the things around us, is a very handy notion. It is not a bad approximation to how things are, and it greatly simplifies dealing with the basics of life: survival, reproduction, not getting hit by buses— things like that. That may be why we human beings do it: it has evolutionary survival value. Certainly the unfortunate people who fail to develop a sense of self (like those who fail to develop a sense of things) have a much harder time of life than those of us who acquire a nice, solid sense of 'being me.'

However, the fact that having a sense of self is a handy approximation to truth does not make it true in an ultimate sense. And since Buddhism is interested in helping people get as close to truth as they possibly can, approximations aren't good enough. For this purpose, the useful notion of a self gets in the way of looking clearly at one's experience of existence and of seeing it for exactly what it is: always changing, always flowing, never the same from one instant to another. In other words, Buddhism holds that you and I are simply ideas and names which we superimpose on the more fundamental experience of flow. We are convenient fictions, just like things are; we have no more reality than this book has. Sorry about that.

All of this becomes more and more real as a person puts the Eightfold Path into practice. This business about the self not being real is not just a mental exercise: it has important consequences for how people live their lives. This is because the belief in a self tends to form the nucleus around which we form all sorts of other beliefs and attachments. The faster horses, wilder lovers, older whiskey, and more money are all *for me*. If I am just a changing flux of consciousness, then what's the point of getting faster horses? Which is exactly the point: to see through the fiction of a self is to undercut the basis for attachments. That makes them a whole lot easier to give up, and *that* makes for a much less unhappy life.

But this isn't all: to the extent that we loosen up our grip on a self, we see that you and I are actually part of something larger: we're both part of the same wonderful flow of space/time/being that everything is. This sense of oneness acts to deepen an individual's empathy for other people and for all creatures. A person understands and experiences in a new way just how much it hurts inside when he or she harms someone else. Letting go of the notion of a separate self did not create this interconnectedness: it was always there. But it does enable one to be more acutely aware of it. And by becoming aware of just how interconnected we really are, a whole new level of insight opens up as to the causes of our core unhappiness. In addition to being aware of the unhappiness that arises from holding onto desires, a person has a new appreciation of just how much unhappiness comes from hurting other beings. The two are connected, of course, because most of us don't really hurt others simply for the fun of it; we hurt them either because we think it is necessary in order to get something or because we are acting under the influence of the intoxicants of anger or delusion. This insight into just how powerfully we are all interconnected is the reason why the Eightfold Path speaks so much about refraining from harming others; it is also why some traditions of Buddhist teaching pay as much attention to living an ethical life as they do to giving up attachments.

There is yet another consequence to allowing the notion of a self to drop away: joy. It is a joy that is somehow related to a sense of having come home, of being where one has always belonged, of waking up from the bad dream of ultimate aloneness. As time and practice of the Eightfold Path go on, it gradually dawns on a person that this feeling, which was first experienced as joy because it was so new and different, is really simply the natural state of our mind when we stop separating ourselves from the unborn, undying, ever-flowing nature of the universe.

Putting all of this together, it becomes clear that there are actually four ways in which attachments cause us to live in chronic unhappiness and dissatisfaction:

- desire is painful, in and of itself;
- because of the changing nature of the world, desires are guaranteed to lead to frustration;
- in the process of trying to force the world to fulfill our desires, we tend to harm others, which in turn is painful to us; and

- desires are what cement in place the notion of a self, which then separates us from the oneness of our true nature, and that separation is an unhappy state to be in.

This, then, is a more complete understanding of the Second Noble Truth that the cause of core unhappiness is attachment, desire, or clinging. It explains more about why Buddhism places such importance on this principle and why the steps of the Eightfold Path are as they are.

What About the Soul?

If Buddhism concludes that there really isn't a semi-permanent sort of a self, an obvious next question to ask is whether it believes in an immortal soul. And it's not too hard to guess what Buddhism has to say about that: no soul, either. A soul is sort of like an eternal self, and the things that suggest there is no self apply to the soul as well. The experience of Buddhists through the centuries has been that, as more and more attachments are given up, and as one gets ever closer to seeing the universe as an immaculately void flow of space/time/being, there is less of a need for (and also less of a basis for) a belief in an immortal soul. This is a very radical conclusion for a religion to make, and it is one of the things which distinguishes Buddhism from all of the other great religions of the world.

Of course, if there is no soul there can't very well be an eternal afterlife for the soul to dwell in, and Buddhism dispenses with that belief as well. When one first hears of it, this idea can be quite worrisome. Does it mean, for example, that Buddhists believe that after death there is *nothing*? No, not nothing; just *no thing*. Since no thing and no one is ever really apart from the unformed, uncreated, undying, unconditioned nature of the flow of space/time/being itself, we always have been, and always will be, one with it. Death can, and will, make big changes in the body, mind, and consciousness which we like to think of as ourself, but death is quite irrelevant to the fact of our oneness with the flow. It is this Buddhists take comfort in, rather than in an eternal continuation of the self in the form of a soul, when faced with the uncertainties of death.

The principle of there being no soul is actually so fundamental to Buddhism that it is given a name ('anatta'), and placed on the same level of importance as the principle of universal change ('anicca'). It is regarded, in other words, as a basic property of how the universe works. Although the first thing that we tend to think of when confronted with the concept of there being no soul is its implications for death and the afterlife, it actually has consequences that are more far-reaching than that.

One of these consequences has to do with just how much 'at one' we really are with the flow. A soul, being inherently a separate sort of a thing, would actually place a limit upon that oneness. No soul and no self, no limit. *If neither self nor soul is ultimately real, then in truth we are, right at this very moment, completely one with the unborn, undying, unformed nature of reality, whether we recognize and experience this or not.* Now, various schools of Buddhism do different things with this fact of absolute oneness. Some simply observe that it exists, while others give it a name and a prominent place in their teaching, using words such as, "we are all Buddha", or "all people have Buddha Nature." Its place in their teaching is both as a cornerstone for faith and as a guide for practice. It acts as a cornerstone for faith in that, to the extent that one can trust in the truth of it (even when that truth is not always evident), it helps a person to keep going through the many difficulties we inevitably encounter in life. It helps a person to keep perspective, to keep the 'big picture' in mind, and not to fret too much about how long it takes to let go of all those cravings and intoxications.

As a guide to practice, the understanding that we all have Buddha Nature influences practice away from trying to get something (to achieve a goal of nirvana, for instance) and towards removing the obstacles to realizing what we already have. This is an important but subtle shift. So long as one is doing Buddhist practice as a means to a goal, the effort is inevitably tainted with some degree of desire: a very noble desire, but a desire nonetheless. Furthermore, it is quite difficult to stop from guessing about what it will be like when that goal is realized. And since such guesses are necessarily inaccurate, all they do is produce yet another false idea to clutter up our poor old minds. When an individual adopts the view that he or she is already innately Buddha, all of this can be dropped and practice can be done simply for the sake of practice. Such a person can just do what needs to be done for no other reason than it is…what needs to be done. This gets back to the 'goal of goallessness' that was mentioned in the section on right effort.

Another consequence of the principle of no soul is that where there is no soul there can be no sin. Many religions define sin as the deliberate turning of the soul away from God, but if there is no soul, that can't happen. And if we are inherently one with everything and we are Buddha by nature, what can be turned away from? The absence of a sense of sin is another major difference between Buddhism and most other great religions of the world, and it has many implications. If there is no sin and no soul, there can be no guilt, no judgement, no atonement, no absolution, no damnation, no salvation. There really can't even be any such thing as evil, in the way it is normally thought of.

In place of all this, for Buddhists, there are simply actions and their natural consequences. There are complex chains of cause and effect, each cause having its own reasons for being, and each action having its inevitable effects, as determined by the way the universe works. When a person engages in some action which is harmful to self or others, it eventually becomes a cause for profound sorrow and regret. Harmful action is regarded by the Buddhist as a mistake. Not having the concepts of sin, guilt, or evil can make the regret for these mistakes a little easier to bear; not having a concept of absolution can make it last a little longer.

The response to having made a mistake is, for the Buddhist, more a question of seeking to understand the causes of one's actions, and then of doing something to change them, rather than a question of finding the root of evil within oneself and removing it.

Looking closely at the causes of harmful acts, what one sees are the chains of multiple, interacting previous causes mentioned above. But what lies at the heart of these; what was the 'first cause,' so to speak? Here is where we are likely to find evil, if it truly exists. Surprisingly, what Buddhists seem to find when they trace the causes of harmful acts all the way back to their source is not evil but purity. There is usually a pure motive, coupled with a sad lack of understanding of how the world works. An example of this was given earlier, when the nature of what lies beneath anger was discussed. But it is not just angry acts that have pure intentions at their core; all harmful acts seem to have this property, when one looks deeply enough into them.

The pure motives are generally pretty simple ones: love, compassion, wanting the best for our family, our people, our nation, our religion, etcetera. When coupled with ignorance of how things work, however, these pure motives lead to unwise actions, which bring unintended painful consequences. This pain then twists and distorts the motives, which leads to even more unwise actions, and so forth until what eventually results are such things as hatred, bigotry, cruelty, fanaticism, bloodshed, etcetera. While these give a pretty good appearance of being evil, when a person looks at them in this way, they are seen as just the terribly sad consequences of ignorance having twisted up pure motives. From this, one can conclude that acts such as rooting out or punishing evil, whether that evil is within oneself or others, are part of the problem rather than being a realistic solution. Seen through Buddhist eyes, they look like a compounding of delusion.

The emphasis in Buddhism on ignorance instead of evil as an explanation for human behavior helps to explain why the step of right understanding is such an important part of the Eightfold

Path. It also makes a large difference in how Buddhists tend to approach life's problems, both their own and those of society. They tend to favor the gentle approach: education, careful investigation, moral persuasion, praise for things well done, and nonviolent social action, rather than the use of force, moral condemnation, or punishment. There are, of course, plenty of times when this is lost sight of, and so there are plenty of exceptions to it, but it helps to explain the observation made by historians that countries which are primarily Buddhist seem to be a little less warlike than the average.

These are some of the radically different ways of looking at the world, and of living within it, which occur as a natural consequence of putting into practice the basic principles of the Law of Change, the Four Noble Truths, and the Eightfold Path. But these are not the only ones. Others arise when the Buddhist looks closely at the nature of cause and effect.

5.
Laws of the Universe

The idea that actions have natural consequences is central to the way Buddhists view the world. In fact, everything that has been discussed so far can be looked at as being a simple function of natural laws of cause and effect. This includes the operation of the Law of Change and the tendency for the practice of the Eightfold Path to produce good effects, as well as the propensity for attachment to lead to suffering. In addition to these natural principles, there are five general types of cause and effect which have been recognized by Buddhism as governing how things work in the universe. To view the world through Buddhist eyes is to see these sets of natural laws at work. When a person does this, it produces some surprising additional changes in how things look.

Physical Cause and Effect

Interestingly enough, the first of these groups of laws of the universe corresponds roughly to what modern science would regard as the laws of the inorganic sciences (physics, chemistry, astronomy, etcetera). This is not to say that early Buddhism actually divided up the world in quite the same way that modern science does, nor that Buddhist writers have generally concerned themselves with the specifics of these sciences. However, some form of recognition that natural laws exist in the physical realm goes all the way back to the beginnings of Buddhism.

Among these laws of cause and effect, Buddhism has traditionally recognized such things as gravity, the nature of energy, seasonal variations in the earth's climate, and the interrelation of wind, rain, and temperature. These have been collectively referred to as 'utu niyama,' the order of the seasons, and they are regarded as laws which are not subject to human alteration. Buddhists hold that people can change our world by operating within these laws, but we cannot change the laws themselves.

Biological Cause and Effect

Another group of natural laws recognized by the Buddhist religion is called the 'order of germs and seeds' ('bija niyama'). Here we find principles which would be recognized by modern science as belonging to biology and its related fields. It may be interesting to present-day biologists that early Buddhists recognized that principles of genetics were particularly important; most of the ancient discussions of biological laws described the resemblance between parents and offspring in humans, animals, and plants.

Mental Cause and Effect

This category of universal laws is not quite as simple as the first two. It covers not only social and psychological principles but also things which Western thought would classify as parapsychology and mystical religion. For the sake of clarity, I will take some liberties with the traditional classification here, and I will go into the religious section of this category when I describe the final set of laws, which are mostly related to spiritual matters. It is noteworthy, however, that early Buddhism recognized that some religious principles were closely related to how peoples' minds work.

The non-religious aspects of the mental category include such things as how consciousness arises and how it works, how thoughts arise, and how thoughts influence behavior. It also includes a parapsychological component: things like mental telepathy, premonition, and other mental events which modern science has trouble evaluating. Traditional Buddhist thought accepts the existence of these psychic events in a rather matter-of-fact sort of a way, and then it steers the follower of the Path away from them, holding that they are largely irrelevant to real spiritual development and a potential source of distraction, intoxication, and similar mischief. In general, classical Buddhism recognizes that the mind has its own set of laws, called 'the order of the mind' or 'citta niyama,' which are just as natural and just as orderly as the laws governing physics and biology.

Buddhism's long history of acknowledging the validity of what would be called today 'scientific laws,' without becoming highly involved in the specifics of what they are, has created for the religion a unique relationship to modern science: one of respect, without a high degree of involvement. In fact, the classic writings on the subject teach that religious speculation about these natural laws, particularly about such things as how the world began and how it would end, is a waste of time. Concentrate on understanding and accepting what *is*, these teachings say, and leave what 'may have been' and 'might become' to others. Since the religion has not concerned itself with the validity of any particular cosmology or other scientific theory, it has not tied the status of its own world view to them, and it has no particular stake in their current state of acceptance. In this way, Buddhism has generally escaped the conflicts with science which have been a feature of many Western religions, and it can afford to adopt the position that anything which leads to truth is good Buddhism. In consequence, Buddhist societies tend to place a high value on secular education, while at the same time reminding people that there is more to life than what pure reason can know.

Ethical Cause and Effect

Now, this comfortable relationship between Buddhism and science is rather convenient for Westerners who have an intellectual outlook on life and who may be looking for a religion which does not conflict with that. In fact, Buddhism does tend to be somewhat popular with such folks. Being a 'recovering intellectual,' this is what attracted me to the religion. But Buddhism also says that there are two more types of natural law, and this is where things start to get, well…interesting. The rest of this chapter is an attempt to convey an intuitive understanding of these two. In order to do this it will be necessary here, even more than in the rest of the book, to set aside scholarship and go into a way of speaking which is intuitive. This means that what follows is more a personal understanding than a summary of classic Buddhist teaching. The conclusions that are drawn are (hopefully) pure, standard Buddhism, but the way in which I am going to get there is not the way in which it is usually done. The difficulty with 'the way in which it is usually done' is that it involves simply stating the Buddhist doctrine about these things as fact, and that is all. That approach doesn't seem terribly helpful to Westerners who are encountering this material for the first time.

One of these last two types of natural laws deals with the area of the consequences of ethical and unethical actions. A person can start to get a feel for this area by first returning to the observation that it hurts when we harm others. Why this natural human empathy exists, from a scientific point of view, I do not know: the point is that it is so. There are a number of interesting features of the inner pain which is caused by doing harm to others. One is that it is roughly in proportion to the harm we cause: small harm, small pain; big harm, big pain. Another is that it sort of waits around to be felt. If we block it out at the time that we are causing the damage, we still feel it later, even many years later, when we allow ourselves to look at what we've done. That brings up another characteristic: this empathic pain seems to require that we face up to what we've done before we can be fully free of it. It is as if the pain is trying to teach us something, and only when we have fully accepted what happened, learned the lesson of empathy, and resolved to do things differently—only then does it really leave us alone. And a further feature of this type of pain is that, after its work is done, it ends; it really is gone. Something has been set to rest in a profound way.

There seems to be no way around feeling this kind of distress, if the harm has been significant. Small harms sometimes produce pains which will simply fade over the course of time, even if they are not faced squarely; but large ones seem to demand the process of accepting and learning from what was done. At first glance, it seems like all of this is just a simple observation that people feel bad if they hurt one another, but that is just the tip of the iceberg. When the acts of harm are substantial, this pain runs very deep and has profound effects on a person's life. The more we put the matter off, the worse it hurts: it is almost as if the act of trying to avoid facing ourselves adds additional pain. This actually makes sense, since the act of avoidance strengthens a delusion in the person doing the avoiding, and this itself is harmful. Therefore, since avoiding things causes more harm, it might be expected to bring about further feelings of suffering.

Yet another interesting property of this sort of empathic pain is that a person's motivations matter. While harmful actions done with good motives are not free of painful consequences, the distress which comes when the motives were good is much less than what comes when the motives were selfish. I am speaking here of the immediate motives; what I've said is not in conflict with the notion spoken about earlier, that if we dig deeply enough and go back far enough, pure motives will be found behind almost every chain of hurtful cause and effect.

When a person starts to face up to what he or she has done, there is both remorse and also a need to feel, in some way, what it was like to be the one who was harmed. Learning to accept the full feeling of empathy seems to be a part of what this process is about, and since empathy is an aspect of wisdom and enlightenment, this means that the process is one which encourages people to grow up, to mature spiritually. It is not simply a sort of punishment which we inflict upon ourselves subconsciously: it is a benevolent process in which our personal pain teaches lessons which cause us to become more compassionate and wise. And so, over the course of time and over the sum of all people, it leads very gradually towards less harm being done in the world.

Another encouraging thing about all this is that it appears to have a positive counterpart: helping others makes us feel good. Again, we may not really know why it happens, but most of us have felt the sort of quiet joy which comes from doing things that benefit others. And, interestingly enough, this positive causal link has some things in common with the negative one. Little benefit, little joy; large benefit, large joy. Again, motives matter: a selfish reason for a beneficial action doesn't destroy the resulting joy altogether, but it certainly reduces it considerably.

Like the pain, the joy seems to wait around, but it does so in a different way. It often is felt at the time of being helpful, then seems to go away for long periods, only to reappear at crucial times in a person's life. People who have been brought back from the edge of dying often report that one of the things which made a big impression on them was how they were shown all the little acts of kindness they'd done in their life, and how important such seemingly little things were. It is as if the merit of benevolent acts is stored up somehow, ready for when we need it most, whereas the pain of unkind acts continues only for so long as we refuse to face up to ourselves.

Again, the simple fact of feeling good when you help someone is but the tip of the iceberg. Another similarity between the positive and negative sides of this process of cause and effect in the ethical realm is that they both appear to be leading humanity towards compassion and wisdom. Our human nature, which wants to avoid pain and seek pleasure, may be what leads us into the mess of seemingly endless frustration and unhappiness, but it is also somehow being used to get us out of the mess by leading us away from selfishness and towards benevolence, simply because the one feels bad and the other feels good. And since Buddhism holds that benevolence is one of the signs of enlightenment, this means that both sides of the process are leading the whole world towards enlightenment, very slowly and very gently.

There is a name which is given to this sort of causal link between people's actions and how they feel. The name is 'karma,' and it is probably the most misunderstood term in the Buddhist religion. When people hear the word 'karma,' they tend to think of fate or destiny, in the sense of some mysterious force which controls a person and about which nothing can be done. But the exact opposite is true: karma is a natural consequence of what we do, and therefore it can be changed by simply doing things differently.

Sometimes people say, "It is my karma to act this way," as if karma is what causes them to do things. But the process that has just been described does not result in actions, it produces feelings. *Every intentional action which has any ethical component at all— every action which results in any harm or benefit to anything whatsoever—produces either negative or positive karma, which in turn ripens into painful or pleasurable feelings for the person who engaged in that action.* If, instead of resulting in feelings, karma could directly cause actions, a never-ending cycle would result: one action causes karma, which causes another action, which causes more karma, which causes more actions, etcetera. This would result in complete determinism and the destruction of people's ability to do anything to change their lives, which is totally contrary to what Buddhism is all about. Of course, people's habitual actions will influence them in ways which make other actions more likely. But those types of causal link are not inescapable fate, and they have as much to do with the laws of psychology as they do with karma.

Another common misconception about karma is that it makes events happen, i.e. that it causes such things as automobile accidents, illness, or death. Some people even take this position so far that they believe there is no point in being careful on the road or seeing a doctor, because "if it is my karma to die now, it will happen; and if not, it won't." This type of fatalism is regarded by Buddhist teachers as a delusion, an excuse not to take responsibility for one's actions. It must be a delusion because, if it were true, it would lead to complete nonsense. For instance, if karma caused death, then, since it is possible to clean up all of one's karma (arahants do that), the world should be littered with thousand-year-old Buddhist saints. But it isn't; they all get sick and die despite having no karma left. Or, if karma could cause (or prevent) car crashes, then it must have the power to control the laws of physics that deal with velocity, momentum, etcetera. And if that were true, then people could control the physical universe simply by creating good or bad karma. Nothing of the sort happens.

All that karma does is to connect our *actions* with our subsequent *feelings*. Of course, our actions have all sorts of other consequences as well, so they actually do influence things like whether we have an accident or get ill, but they do this through the laws of physics and biology and psychology, not through karma. Buddhism sees the law of karma as being opportunistic: *it works through the other laws of nature rather than controlling them.* The pain of a car wreck or a disease may, therefore, provide the opportunity for a person to experience something akin to what they may have inflicted upon someone else in the past, and to learn from it. But that is a whole different thing from the karma having caused the disease.

So far, I have discussed karma in terms of cause and effect over the course of a person's life. While this may be a somewhat difficult notion for we Westerners to accept, it is not nearly as weird as the concept of karma extending over many lives. And Buddhists do speak of it in just those terms. When they do, it often sounds like they believe that a person is reincarnated after death, to pick up the karma of his or her past deeds and continue training with it in the next life, life after life, until enlightenment is reached. Even if people can get their heads around the idea that reincarnation might actually happen, there is still a big problem with this: *what gets reincarnated*? If I have lived before and will live again, it sure sounds like there is a 'me' that exists and that I'm a fairly permanent sort of a thing. In other words, if reincarnation happens, there must be a self and a soul to be reincarnated. But that runs squarely against the Buddhist principle of anatta: there's no real self and no real soul. What's wrong here?

What is wrong is that what I just said about reincarnation is an older and simpler view than what Buddhism teaches. It is actually closer to Hinduism than to Buddhism. Hinduism is another of the world's great religions, even older than Buddhism, and it forms part of the religious background out of which Buddhism grew, sort of like the way Christianity and Islam grew out of the background of the older religion of Judaism. In the Hindu belief, there is a separate soul which does reincarnate life after life until it finally wins rest in union with God. The Buddhist view is more complex than this.

Please understand that what you are about to read is only one approach to understanding the rebirth side of karma: once again I am branching out on my own, to try to open a door to something. And once again I am pointing at something which is not fully capable of being described in words nor known to the intellect. I'll start by accepting the idea that there really is no such thing as a self or a soul. If that is so, then when an empathic connection is established between two people in this lifetime by one harming the other and then feeling the other's pain, where might that connection, that karma, exist? It can't reside within either person, because there actually aren't two people: 'people' is just a shortcut way of talking about it. The karma must dwell in the only thing which really does exist, the endless flow of space/time/being.

Think of the karma as a disturbance within that flow, a disturbance created by the destructive act.

Such disturbances tend to persist, if they are big enough, until an act of compassion and empathy sets them to rest. But what happens if a disturbance is not set to rest within the lifetime of the people involved in its creation? Suppose, since the flow of space/time/being is endless and timeless, that the disturbance continues after their deaths. How might it be set to rest, and why might it continue onwards in the first place? One way for it to be set to rest would be for some future person to become so closely joined with that disturbance that he or she could feel the pain. Then that new individual could learn from it how to avoid making the same mistake in his or her own life. In this way the empathy and compassion of this new individual would set the old karma to rest. And even though the original person failed to learn from his or her mistake, someone else did; that makes the mistake less likely to be repeated in the future, since there is one more person who knows better. This means that the pain of humanity's past mistakes would never be wasted, and we would continue to progress, ever so slowly, towards enlightenment. It would imply that we live in an incredibly compassionate and loving universe which, simply by the operation of its natural laws of cause and effect, enfolds into itself the suffering of each wounded being and patiently turns even the most horrendous of our errors towards the good. And this would be the reason why disturbances continue onward within the flow until their lesson is learned by someone, somewhere.

In all of this explanation, there has been no need to assume that a soul is born again into a new body. All that is needed is for some new person to become intimately connected with the ongoing disturbance in space/time/being left behind by another person who died before learning from his or her mistakes. *It is, in other words, the karma (the disturbance) that lives on, not the person.* And this karma becomes connected with the new person in such an intimate way that it conditions their whole being. How that connection forms is not fully understood, but it seems to happen very early in life, probably well before birth. However it may happen, the result is sometimes so powerful that it *feels almost as if* the new person were a continuation of the old one, but not quite. Sometimes the link is so strong that a person can even 'remember' one or more 'past lives.' And sometimes it seems good to speak in terms of past lives and rebirth, even though these short-cut ways of speaking make it seem like we are saying that a particular being had lived before. Buddhist teachers sometimes speak that way, because they have to use ordinary language to get their points across to people. The cost of this, of course, is that it can cause confusion.

And it has done just that. It would not be uncommon to pick up a Buddhist book and read that if a person does a certain thing in this lifetime, karma will cause a certain other thing to happen to them in a future life. This is what might be called the 'Sunday school' level of Buddhism, and it has its uses. What I have tried to convey is closer to the 'theological school' level, which is more subtle and complex. In understanding karma at this level, it helps to keep reminding oneself that it is the karma that is reborn, not the person (some Buddhists use the term 'rebirth,' to distinguish what is being talked about from the Hindu concept of 'reincarnation'). And it is reborn by *influencing* the existence of a new being, not by *creating* it; the actual creation of the new being would be a matter of the natural biological laws.

I say a new 'being' because Buddhism expands the scope of the process of rebirth to include animals and various spiritual beings. Anything, in other words, will be made use of by the ultimately compassionate force of karma. Anything whatsoever, which can be of use in setting past torment to rest and in bringing the world forward towards enlightenment, will be used.

Seen in this way, the law of karma is so beautifully benevolent that some Buddhists take a vow not to set themselves apart from it, by entering nirvana, until all humanity is enlightened. This is called the 'Bodhisattva Vow,' and it is characteristic of Mahayana Buddhism, one of the two great families within the religion. The Zen schools, one of which I belong to, are part of this Mahayana family. An individual who makes this offering to set aside the final fulfillment of their own enlightenment in order that all may enter enlightenment together, is said to practice the Bodhisattva Path. 'Bodhisattva' simply means 'a being of enlightenment.' Of course, since there is no soul to be reborn from one life to another, this way of practice cannot involve a person actually reappearing, as the same entity, from one lifetime to another, in order to serve humanity. And it certainly does not mean that people deliberately leave bits of negative karma unresolved, so that something gets reborn. Instead, it has to do with the positive side of karma, and it involves a resolve to set aside everything, even one's own final enlightenment, in order to be of service to the operation of a compassionate universe.

The other great family of Buddhism, the Theravada or 'Way of the Elders,' stresses each person going forward unrelentingly towards enlightenment. This is also deeply meaningful, for if each person does not do this, who will? Scholars and relatively new Buddhists sometimes discuss the differences between these two great families and argue about which offers the better way. Experienced practitioners of both ways tend to get along very well with each other and just smile a little sadly at the arguments. Perhaps this is because there is something greater that they both share, in the face of which the discussions and arguments seem to pale in importance. Perhaps it is because both ways converge upon a very similar place. How can one truly be of benefit to all beings unless one has unrelentingly practiced the Path to awakening; how could one practice that Path in earnest and fail to have it result in a profound wish to benefit all beings?

The operation of karma in influencing the birth of a new being is one way in which disturbances in the flow of space/time/being can be set to rest. There appears to be another way, as well. This alternate way operates through the positive side of karma: that benevolent acts have merit and lead to positive feelings. I use the word 'merit' deliberately: it is one of the alternate names for positive karma. It has already been said that some of the things which are true of negative karma are also true of positive karma or merit, and that there are a few big differences. One difference that has already been mentioned is that merit seems somehow to be stored up until it is needed. Another is that, unlike negative karma, merit can be offered to others; it can be transferred.

Now, a property of all karmas, both positive and negative, is that they can interact. Therefore, merit can neutralize, or at least soften to some extent, the course of negative karma. And, another characteristic of karma is that, if the lesson which needs to be learned from negative karma can be learned in some way other than by re-experiencing the pain of past mistakes, then there is no need for the pain to come up at all: it is simply washed away. This is another aspect of the compassionate nature of the whole process.

When we put all of this together, an interesting picture develops: it is possible to set negative karma to rest by one person offering the merit of his or her own religious training to others. This has been done since the beginning of Buddhism. One of the earliest ceremonies developed by Buddhists was for the offering of merit to the dead. Again, a short-cut way of speaking has just been used. Since there's no soul being reincarnated, there's no point in offering merit to something that isn't there in the first place. But while 'the dead' may not be there in a strict sense, the unresolved negative karma of what they did continues on as a disturbance. Those who are alive can help set that disturbance to rest by offer-ing the merit of their own benevolent acts; they can also help by offering the merit of their own practice of the Way, wherein the lessons of how to live an ethical life are learned.

Throughout this discussion of karma, I have pointed out a number of possible misunderstandings. Such misunderstandings are not new: Buddhist teachers and scholars were trying to address the very ones I mentioned, as early as the Council of Patna in 246 B.C.E.! The reason for emphasizing them here is that how a Buddhist understands this aspect of his or her religion makes quite a difference. Karma, if understood accurately, leads to compassion and personal responsibility; understood carelessly, it can lead to all sorts of trouble. Take, for example, the mistaken notion that rebirth implies the existence of a soul. The consequence of this view tends to be that people either reject the whole idea of karma as being unnecessary or perhaps even un-Buddhist, or they start holding onto a notion that somehow there really is a 'me,' after all. Both of these are unfortunate, as they restrict a person's ability to see the full picture of how Buddhism understands the universe.

Another example of the trouble caused by misunderstandings about karma is that some Buddhist cultures have taken a callous attitude towards people who are ill, disabled, impoverished, etcetera, because of a simplistic belief that such people deserve their misfortunes and that there's nothing that can be done about it anyway. On a personal level, some people take a similar position about themselves, feeling that if they are ill, for example, it means that they are suffering some sort of cosmic punishment for having been bad and that to seek medical treatment would be to refuse to accept their karmic 'fate.' Hopefully, I have shown the ways in which these views are misguided, and how they run squarely against the basic principles of enlightenment.

The reverse of these mistakes is also made: people sometimes assume that because they are training in the Path, the merit of this will protect them from the consequences of any unethical actions, and they can therefore get up to almost anything. When acted upon, this view tends to produce a lot of suffering quite quickly, sometimes for people in addition to themselves. It is a sad way to learn about how karma really works! The merit of sincere religious training is undoubtedly great, and it can interact with the negative karma which a person makes. But it does not completely eliminate it in some mechanical sort of a way that can be taken for granted. Furthermore, motivations matter a lot in this business, so someone who does benevolent acts in a calculating way, figuring that this will let them escape the consequences of their harmful acts, is in for a rude awakening. And, since karma, even positive karma, does not control the other laws of the universe, people will still reap the natural physical, biological, and psycho-social consequences of whatever they do.

The law of ethical cause and effect, which is referred to as 'karma niyama' or the 'order of acts and their consequences,' when understood in its subtlety, not only helps people make sense of a universe which sometimes seems cruel and meaningless, but it also leads them onwards in compassion and in taking full responsibility for their actions.

Spiritual Cause and Effect

This last of the five classes of natural laws refers to something that is a bit hard to describe. It is called 'Dharma niyama,' the 'order of the norm,' and it could be summarized by saying that the universe itself is of a spiritual or religious nature, or that in the *very* long run all things tend towards enlightenment, or that each person is somehow touched by truth and drawn towards it. These statements sound like a simplistic belief that everything is for the best, but that is not what is meant. Buddhism definitely acknowledges the deep suffering which exists in our world, the great sadness of the mistakes which people make, and the profoundly damaging consequences which some of these have. And yet…. It is the 'and yet' to which this last group of laws refers. And yet—somehow—things don't stay that way. And yet—somehow—truth prevails in the end. And yet—somehow—it is impossible to kill the human spirit. And yet—somehow—ignorance does not triumph in the long run. A *very long term* point of view is needed to see this, and this group of laws suggests that Buddhists cannot afford to be impatient, short-sighted, or intolerant. But more than this, it suggests that they actually can afford to take the risk of being both patient and tolerant since, in the end, time and the very nature of the universe are on the side of what is good.

Perhaps what underlies some of these natural spiritual laws is the simple fact that reliable and stable truths actually do exist in this world of constant flux. As mentioned earlier, one of the things which enlightenment teaches people is that there really is something stable and reliable within the flow of the universe. Not some-*thing*, but something: that which is described as being unborn, uncreated, and unconditioned—truth itself. If this is really the way things are, the consequences are quite revolutionary and optimistic. Since delusion, addiction, pain, ignorance, attachment, etcetera, are born, created, and conditioned, then by their very nature they are unstable. And since basic truth is unborn, uncreated, and unconditioned, then by its very nature it is stable.

The implication is clear: over extremely long periods of time it is to truth that humankind will return. It is inevitable; it is a mathematical certainty, if you like. All the rest keeps changing: we can dash back and forth from one untruth to another for ages, but it is theoretically impossible to stay with any one of them forever. Eventually people have to encounter simple, stable truths. Truth is, if you will, the default setting of the universe. If we add to this the compassionate and loving nature of the universe as seen in moments of enlightenment, and even as reflected in something as apparently stern as the law of karma, a world view begins to emerge which is very heartening indeed. Far from seeing the world as simply suffering, through Buddhist eyes it actually looks like an ongoing evolution towards truth and enlightenment. And this is visible on both a personal and a universal scale. All of this does not mean that human beings can afford to sit back and fail to do what must be done. Quite the contrary, it means that each moment is an opportunity not to be wasted, an opportunity to take our small but essential part in the greatest adventure of them all: the positive spiritual evolution of the universe.

6.
So, Is This a Religion?

We are almost at the end of a book on religion and nothing much has been said about God, faith, and worship: things which are basic to most religions. It kind of makes a person wonder if Buddhism is actually a religion, after all. Or is it more like an unusually complete philosophy of life? This question is something which scholars of religion, and Buddhists themselves, have debated. Most books on comparative religion include it as one of the world's great religions, and probably the majority of Buddhists also think of it that way. So do I. But please decide for yourself.

If it is a religion, it is certainly a somewhat odd one: no soul, no sin, no eternal afterlife, no story of creation nor view about the end of the world. Instead, what it seems to have is just this incredibly loving universe, with a bunch of natural laws operating without much sign of a Creator, each person bearing an individual responsibility to follow a Path towards enlightenment. So, if there is to be a basis for deciding whether or not Buddhism is a religion, it might be helpful to have a look at how it relates to those more usual elements of world religions: God, faith or belief, and worship.

The God Element

God was important in the Hindu religion from which Buddhism developed. There was both one Supreme Being and also many lesser gods. But Buddhist teaching does not often mention these. For this reason, some people in the West have concluded that Buddhism is actually atheistic: that it denies the existence of God. Actually, that is not what it does, and its teachings do from time to time mention both the Supreme God of the Hindus and some of the lesser ones as well. What Buddhism has done might actually be even more radical than atheism: it acknowledges the existence of God and the gods, and then treats them as not being all that important.

In the Buddhist view, any God (in the sense of an individual, personal Supreme Being) which exists must be subject to the same laws of the universe that everything else is. Since the Buddhist world view does not require a Creator God, Who stands outside of the universe, Buddhism treats the Hindu Supreme Being (and, by implication, any other God) as being as much a part of the natural universe as we are. God, in this view, is subject to change, and He does not have the power to alter fundamental natural laws. In other words, while Buddhist teachings do not deny the existence of a God, they do deny His omnipotence, omnipresence, and omniscience. An implication of this would be that no God has the ability to bring a person to nirvana through His grace alone. While God, or the gods, may indeed be of help, each person is still responsible for doing what is necessary for his or her own spiritual development. And it is for this reason that Buddhist teachings focus on what we can do about ourselves rather than on how we relate to a Supreme Being.

Admittedly, this sounds pretty close to atheism, since most other religions would probably maintain that a god that is neither all powerful, all knowing, nor ever-present simply isn't God. But it is not that simple, for, if Buddhism believes that the universe itself is above God (rather than the other way around), that might mean that the universe *is* God and hence Buddhism is actually a type of pantheism, a religion which identifies God with everything. Here we are into deep theological waters. Because, while the Buddhist teachings assert that a simple belief in, and reliance upon, a Being known as 'God' is not the way to ultimate enlightenment, they also talk about the 'unborn, unbecome, unmade, and unconditioned.' As a matter of fact, the classic texts say that if this did not exist, then no nirvana would be possible and there would be no freedom from the cycle of attachment and frustration. But what, exactly, is this 'unborn, unbecome, unmade, and unconditioned'? About all that I can say is what I've said before: if it is unborn then it is also undying and hence eternal; if it is unbecome and unmade then it is also void of all that can be known or grasped and therefore it is pure and tranquil; if it is unconditioned or uncompounded of other causes then it is complete as it is, pure, and a true refuge. And that is getting to sound rather close to how some folks think of God. Here, as with karma, once the discussion leaves the Sunday school level and enters the subtleties of the theological school level, things start to get delightfully murky.

If I were teaching a theological school seminar on Buddhism, I might continue onwards in this direction, and people could have a fine time discussing how Buddhism really relates to God and whether this 'unborn' business means that Buddhists believe in a 'God the Everything.' While we were at it, we could also debate whether Buddhism, instead of being a religion, is actually a meta-religion: something which attempts to step beyond the boundaries of all religions, whether they be of the One God or of the many gods. It is actually great fun to be around such discussions, especially when old Buddhist and Christian monks, and experienced members of Jewish, Hindu, and Islamic contemplative traditions, get together. Because it is obvious that there is *something* important that they are agreeing upon, despite their differences, even if words ultimately fail them. And the failure of words may be a good part of the problem here. Since both 'God' and 'nirvana' are notorious for being indefinable, it's no wonder that people have a hard time figuring out just how Buddhism relates to God.

Simple statements work all right at the extremes: no, Buddhism is not atheism; no, Buddhism does not worship a Sunday school sort of a God. However, when Buddhist teachers start trying to go further than this in describing the ultimate aspects of their religion, they enter our murky area and hence come up with statements that sound very different from each other. Some will use positive terms such as 'the Unborn,' 'the Eternal,' 'the uncreate,' 'the pure,' 'That Which Is,' 'the absolute,' etcetera. Some, when addressing Western people, will simply use the term that we are used to: 'God.' Others will describe the ultimate in terms of what it is not, and so they will use terms such as 'emptiness,' 'the void,' 'thusness,' or 'cessation.' These sorts of differences can be confusing, but they do not have to be, if we understand that they are simply words: words trying to point at something that is beyond words.

As with all such words, each way of speaking has its costs and its benefits. The positive descriptions give a more definite sense of the 'something,' but they do so at the risk that we will grab onto our ideas about it and conclude that it is 'a thing.' The negative descriptions don't let us make that mistake, but they tempt us to jump to the opposite conclusion: that it's 'a nothing.' Rather than jump to any conclusions, maybe it is better to leave the whole question of the Buddhist view of God in a somewhat murky state. Ultimately that may be closer to the truth than what will happen if we try to force ourselves into coming up with a nice, simple statement that Buddhism does, or does not, believe in God.

The Belief and Faith Elements

I said earlier that one of the unusual things about Buddhism is that it does not require belief from its followers before they can practice it. People are free to rely upon its teachings as a matter of belief if they wish, but before accepting them they can also wait until their own personal experience verifies them. This way is actually recommended as being just as good as the way of belief. One of my favorite passages in the ancient writings is the one where the Buddha was discussing His teaching with a group of rather skeptical village elders. The scene sounded amusingly similar to what one sometimes encounters today: here was yet another holy man coming around and preaching that his way was the true one, and, well…why should we believe him? His response was most refreshing. He told them that their hesitation to simply believe what He said, without a good reason, was sensible. He went on to list a whole number of things that were *not* good reasons for accepting things as being true: tradition, hearsay, simply because they are printed in a book, just because they are logical, because they sound nice, because they agree with your opinions, or because you like the person who is saying them. Instead, He told them, if a particular teaching seems suitable, then try it out and see what happens. If it leads to good results, then place some faith in it and follow it further. If it starts to lead towards unwholesome states of being, then give it up. Pretty practical advice!

While people need not have belief in order to practice Buddhism, they do need a certain amount of faith. Here I am using the term 'belief' in the sense of 'an opinion or conviction which is firmly held without a basis in proof,' and the term 'faith' as being 'trust or confidence in something.' Faith or trust, in this sense, is needed because taking each step in Buddhist training is taking a step into the unknown, and it requires faith to risk doing that. Even if someone goes by the way of direct experience, this trust is an essential part of the process, as you can never fully know where a spiritual path is leading until after you have traveled it. Even if the results have been beneficial so far, that is not complete proof that the next step will not be false.

With time and experience, the Buddhist develops a sort of deep faith or trust in his or her tradition and practice, but this is still not the sort of absolute belief which is characteristic of many religions. Personal religious experience can, and does, lead to confidence and even to certainty about the things which have been confirmed by that experience. Yet, always there is more; always the Path leads onwards into the unknown. In fact, a frequently heard comment among experienced Buddhist trainees is that the farther they go, the more they realize that they do not know. And within this unknowing, both their contentment and their faith grow deeper.

When a person does take Buddhism as a matter of belief, an interesting thing happens. If the individual is to take his or her religion seriously, the life of religious practice which is prescribed by the Eightfold Path must be undertaken. Merely believing in the Path is not sufficient: one has to actually do it. And that practical day-to-day training leads, in time, to experiences which confirm the truth of the teachings which the person first accepted as matters of belief. This means that they are no longer simply beliefs, for there is actual confirmation of them. In other words, it doesn't seem to matter whether a person starts out with belief or without it: eventually both ways of training end up in the same place. It is a place of confidence borne of direct experience, coupled with a deep trust, which leads one ever onwards into the unknown.

In summary, Buddhism is both similar and different to the other great religions of the world with regard to belief and faith. It is different in that belief may, or may not, play a central role in the life of any particular Buddhist. It is similar in that, if the person stays with Buddhist practice for awhile, faith—in the sense of trust—will become a real part of his or her life.

The Worship Element

With regard to worship, Buddhism has yet another paradox to present. On the one hand, the classic Buddhist texts teach that 'reliance upon rites and rituals' is a hindrance to progress on the Path. On the other hand, all one has to do is visit most any Buddhist temple and there will be ceremonies going on, incense burning, flowers and food being offered upon the altar, and at least one statue being bowed to. If that isn't worship, it certainly looks a lot like it.

I would suggest that it really isn't worship after all, at least not in the way the term is generally used. Once again, part of the problem is with words. If by 'worship' we mean 'the ceremonies and other acts which signify reverence and devotion to a deity,' and by which that deity is asked for blessings and help, then that is not quite what is going on in the average Buddhist temple when a ceremony is happening. First of all, Buddhists don't have a deity in the common use of the term. Furthermore, those statues are not quite what they might seem. They are definitely not idols, in the sense of being deities in and of themselves. They are clearly thought of as simply material objects: lumps of wood, metal, stone, etcetera. In fact, there are old stories of priests not hesitating to burn one, or break it up, if people start to believe that the statue itself has god-like or magical powers.

Instead of being idols, each statue is a representation or a reminder of something. The easiest ones to understand are those which represent the figure of the historical Buddha, Shakyamuni. He is represented in a variety of classic poses, with the sitting meditation posture and the standing teaching posture being among the most popular. Artists have not hesitated to portray Him using the facial features of their own race or nation, and so one encounters Shakyamuni Buddha statues which look Indian, Tibetan, Chinese, Japanese, Korean, Vietnamese, Thai, etcetera. The newest, and also the oldest, have Western features. The new ones, of course, are by modern Western artists; the old ones are from the ancient kingdom of Ghandara, which covered parts of what are now western Pakistan and eastern Afghanistan, where the people were of Persian appearance and where classical Greek artistic conventions were in use. Buddhism came to Ghandara in the fourth century B.C.E., and the very first Buddha statues known to have been carved anywhere in the world arose there in the first

Shakyamuni Buddha in standing teaching posture.

century C.E. This sculpture flourished until the decline of Buddhism in this region, in the seventh century C.E. It is these Ghandaran art forms that I have used to illustrate this book.

But what, exactly, is the Buddha who is being represented in these statues? As with many things in Buddhism, there are different levels at which this question can be answered. At the simplest and most straightforward level, the answer is that the Buddha was a historical human being, a person whom Buddhists revere and respect deeply, but do not actually worship.

Although this man was the founder of the Buddhist religion, starting a new religion was not what he set out to do. He was actually searching for an answer to the 'faster horses problem.' It is not a new one: philosophy and religion have been grappling with that problem for as long as recorded history. Many people throughout the ages have recognized this difficulty and tried to do something about it. One of them was a man who lived in northern India some 2500 years ago. His name was Siddhartha Gautama, and he was the crown prince of the small Indian kingdom of the Shakya people on the border of what is now Nepal. And, while there are many wonderful and even miraculous stories about the Buddha's life, there is also plenty of evidence that he was not a god. He was definitely a human being: he had a mother and a father, he was a kid and then a teenager and then an adult, just like you and me. He had the usual aches and pains of a human body, and, at around eighty years of age, he died of what was probably cholera, dysentery, or some similar case of food poisoning. As a youth he was good at sports and martial arts; he was smart, handsome, and popular. As a matter of fact, he was pretty good at just about everything a prince was supposed to do in those days. And that became a problem, because his father, noticing this, became very attached to the idea of having this particular one of his many sons become the next king, and he did all sorts of things to try to make sure that this happened.

Prince Siddhartha.

That was a problem for Prince Siddhartha because he didn't really want to be a king. In the beginning, he wasn't quite sure what he wanted, but he knew that it wasn't to be a king. The trouble was that he was blessed (his father would probably have said 'cursed') with an unusually honest and insightful mind which saw right through most of the comfortable little fictions and distractions that people filled their heads with in those days, just as we still do today. What he saw about himself and the world wasn't pretty: people argued and fought and were never satisfied; when they got what they wanted, they wanted more; no matter what they did, their happiness never seemed to last. And that was just within the gates of his own palace; his father wouldn't let him see what went on outside, since he knew that his son's love for people ran too deep for him to be able to ignore such obvious suffering as poverty, disease, and death. The king figured that if he saw those things, Prince Siddhartha would feel driven to find fundamental answers to why such things took place.

Which is exactly what happened. But unfortunately for his father, things went even worse than he expected, for when the prince finally got outside the gates and saw the full range of life's troubles, he also saw something else: a holy man. From that time onwards there was no longer any question about what he wanted to do with his life. He wanted to be a holy man, too. His father, of course, was completely opposed to this and refused to let him do it. In fact, this had been his father's worst fear all along. At Siddhartha's birth the usual collection of prophets had been assembled to make predictions for his future, and all but one of them had said that the prince would either become a mighty king or else a great holy man. The wisest of them, however, predicted that the prince would leave his throne to become a holy man. To prevent this, the king had tried to keep his son from seeing the real world.

Now that his son had made up his mind, the king tried everything he could think of to keep Siddhartha from doing what his heart desired. He told him that the time was not right: he could be a king first and then retire to be a holy man. He told him that he could do far more good as a king than he ever could hope to do in religion. He worked on his guilt, his loyalty, his sense of patriotism. Each ploy worked for a little while, and, out of respect for his father's wishes, his son would put aside his plan to leave, but his honest mind would not let him do this for long, and once again he would ask his father to let him go. The king even went so far as to arrange a reception for his son with all of the loveliest young noblewomen of the realm, and had his advisors secretly watching which of them Siddhartha seemed most attracted to. A marriage to her was swiftly arranged in hopes that his love for her would keep him at home. But it was all to no avail.

The crisis finally came when Siddhartha's first and only child, Rahula, was born. Realizing that if he stayed any longer his natural fatherly love for his family would make it impossible ever to leave the palace, he made what must have been a gut-wrenching decision: he had his favorite horse saddled and secretly rode out of the palace forever.

He gave up everything for the sake of the truth: his wife and son, his country, power, wealth, his good name, his family and clan—everything. Upon reaching the banks of a great river he stopped, shaved off his hair, and changed his royal clothes for a simple robe. The shaven head and simple robe made of bits and pieces of cast-off cloth were the signs of a holy man in his day, and he kept this appearance for the rest of his life. Twenty-five centuries later, most Buddhist monks still shave their heads and wear some form of this simple robe: these have become the signs of people who are willing to give up everything to follow the Buddha in their search for truth.

Kings, however, do not lose their sons so easily, and Siddhartha was soon found by the king's men. His father then sent a series of royal advisors and priests to try to convince his son to give up the search and return home. The wisest men in the kingdom came to reason with him, but his honest mind saw through their arguments, and none could convince him. Finally his father gave up and left him alone. Now he could devote himself completely to finding truth: to answering the questions that had called to him all this time. Why was he, and everyone around him, never satisfied? Why were people stingy, frustrated, selfish, and cruel? Why did there have to be pain, sickness, despair, even death? And where were the truths which could be relied upon? What was the ultimate nature of reality?

For six years he searched for answers using the ways of the holy men of his time. Two of these ways were to study under the great Hindu priests and the masters of Yoga. These were the main religions of his area, even as they are in India today. He studied with them for several years, mastered their teachings, and learned a great deal from them. Yet, in the end, his basic questions were still not answered; he could sense that there was a level of truth that even they had not reached. And so, he eventually had to set off on his own. He actually didn't want to do that, for he recognized the dangers in having no one to guide him, and he lamented his inability to find a teacher who could guide him the whole way to the ultimate reality. So, he vowed to take truth itself as his teacher, and to respect and serve it as if it were the human teacher whom he lacked. These years of study of Hinduism and Yoga served as the background for his later understanding and practice, and for this reason Buddhism is related to them in a way that is somewhat similar to the way that Christianity is related to Judaism: Buddha was a Hindu and a Yogi, just as Christ was a Jew. Hinduism, Yoga, and Buddhism are still recognized as the family of great religions that started in India, like Judaism, Christianity, and Islam are the family of great religions that started in the Middle East.

Another of the ways which holy men practiced in his day was to put one's body through all sorts of hardships, and Siddhartha tried this practice next. He did this all the way: he endured pain, exposure to the weather, sleeplessness, and starvation.

Siddhartha emaciated due to starvation and ascetic practices.

It actually makes sense that he would think that truth might be found this way: after all, he knew that the soft life of self-indulgence and sensual pleasures that he had known in the palace was a trap; maybe freedom was to be found in its opposite. Unfortunately, it didn't work: all he got was weak, freezing cold or boiling hot, tired, faint, sick, and hungry. He certainly didn't lack courage, for at one point he pushed it so far that he almost died of starvation and was so weak he couldn't even stand. A few of his friends among the holy men had to hold him up.

At this point, something very unusual happened. Some people think of it as a visit by a heavenly being, others as a vision. Whatever it was, he saw one of the guardians of a Hindu heaven playing a three-stringed musical instrument. One string was tuned too loosely and the only sound it could make was something like a 'thunk'; the second was tuned too tightly and so it broke as soon as it was played; the third string was tuned perfectly, and from it came heavenly music. The point got across: truth was not to be found by living the extremes of loose self-indulgence or of tight harshness; there had to be a middle way. That balanced approach to life is still an important part of Buddhism today. Buddhist practice is often called the 'Middle Way,' and its followers try to avoid both the soft life of self gratification and the harsh life of needless self denial. When it comes to finding truth, both of these extremes are traps: they are actually endless distractions. It is just that in the first case you distract yourself with pleasure and your senses, while in the second you distract yourself with pain and your delusions. Neither gets you any closer to seeing clearly what life is really all about.

For Siddhartha at that moment, the middle way was to stop starving himself and get some food; otherwise he was likely to die. And so he accepted a bowl of milk porridge that was offered to him by a passing noblewoman. After eating a proper meal, he felt much stronger in body and mind, but his friends among the holy men were disgusted with him for having 'gone soft,' and so they left him. Now that he was refreshed, clear-headed, and completely alone, he decided to try something very simple: he would sit and meditate under a nearby tree. And he would not use any of the complicated meditation methods he had learned from the Yogis. Instead, he would return to the way he had naturally meditated as a child: he would just sit there comfortably and quietly with his mind alert, aware, and concentrated. He vowed not to rise from under that tree until he had found the answer to his questions. The place where he sat is today a great Buddhist shrine, and a descendent of the original tree grows there still. It is a type of fig tree called a 'bodhi tree,' meaning 'tree of enlightenment,' and its graceful pointed leaves are used by Buddhists as a symbol of their faith.

At first his mind was plagued by every imaginable fear, doubt, desire, lust, distraction, flattery, and lie. But all his previous years of effort, although they had not been able to show him the complete truth, were not in vain. He was able to just keep on sitting there, seeing all these things for the illusions that they were. He neither tried to push them away nor did he get involved with them. He just sat there: calmly, quietly, without fear, without repulsion, without attraction. Eventually all the uproar died down and there was a deep, clear stillness. He kept meditating. Many insights into himself and the world came to his mind as, one by one, the remaining fictions, attachments, and distractions in his head dropped away. He kept meditating. The stillness got deeper and deeper; his mind clearer and clearer, until it became impossible to tell the difference between his mind and the whole universe. He kept meditating. Finally, just before dawn, as the morning star was rising, his very last attachment melted away, *and He knew.*

Or maybe I should say, *He saw*: saw the world with a clear sight, saw it in a way never seen before. Or maybe I should say, *He was, is, and will be the truth, together with the whole universe.* What is being talked about here is something that words aren't too good at describing. Buddhists have words for it, words like 'enlightenment' and 'nirvana', which I have tried to explain earlier, but even these words aren't going to help much because what He realized is something that, by its very nature, goes beyond words. It also goes beyond our thoughts about it, so thinking about it or picturing it in our minds doesn't help a lot either. To really know what the Buddha realized, people have to experience it for themselves. And people do. Because the Buddha was a human being, we too have the potential for doing what He did. While full nirvana, such as the Buddha found that night, is rare in any place or time, many people find smaller and larger 'tastes' of what He found.

From this point until His death some forty-five years later, the Buddha practiced and taught the truths that He realized that night, and this teaching and example became the Buddhist religion. Buddhists refer to Him after this time not by His given name of Siddhartha Gautama, but as Shakyamuni Buddha, 'The Enlightened One of the Shakya Clan.' And many, including myself, use a capital 'H' when referring to Him after His enlightenment, not because He is regarded as God, but out of respect for His being the founder of the faith.

Shakyamuni, then, is the Buddha Whose statues are placed upon temple altars as representations not only of the historical person who started the religion, but also of His teachings, the Path, and all the people who have practiced the Way and passed it down over the centuries: in other words, of the entire religion. Representing these things, the statues act to remind people to be grateful and to inspire them to strive to live up to these examples. Gratitude and inspiration are the purposes of Buddha statues, not worship in the usual sense. And when people bow to these statues, leave donations of food at their feet, or decorate the altar with flowers, these are meant as acts of gratitude and as physical statements of commitment to the Buddha's Way.

In some temples, the only statues you will see are those of Shakyamuni Buddha and perhaps a few of His historical disciples, but in other temples there are a multitude of different statues, some with unusual aspects such as many arms or eyes. Who are they? Some of them represent other Buddhas. The historical Buddha

The Bodhisattva Maitreya, who represents the Buddha who is to come.

did not claim to be the first Buddha ever to exist, and He said that He would not be the last, either. So, some of the statues represent these non-historical Buddhas of the ancient past or of the future. Other statues portray what might be called celestial or transcendent Buddhas. Statues or paintings of these Buddhas tend to be found in temples of the Mahayana family of Buddhism, where they represent large aspects of the Buddha Nature of the universe. One of the most popular, Amitabha Buddha, symbolizes the infinite light of universal Buddhahood. Another, Baisajaya Buddha, personifies the healing aspect of Buddha Nature. Vairocana Buddha, sometimes called the 'Cosmic Buddha,' represents the indefinable Buddhahood of absolutely everything.

Other statues often found in Mahayana temples are of Bodhisattvas, 'beings of enlightenment'; they are representations of the smaller and more personal aspects of Buddha Nature that can be found in individual people rather than in the universe as a whole. Avalokitesvara, for instance, is a very popular figure; she is usually portrayed in female form and symbolizes great compassion. She is the one who often has multiple eyes and arms, to indicate her willingness to see all the needs of the world and to respond to each of them. Prajnaparamita is another Bodhisattva who is usually seen in female form, representing great wisdom. This same virtue is symbolized in male form as the Bodhisattva Manjusri, who is often seen seated upon a ferocious beast—the illusory self. Samantabhadra represents patient spiritual love and rides a great elephant, which itself is symbolic of the unstoppable power that spiritual love exerts upon the world. This Bodhisattva is sometimes portrayed in a form which is hard to recognize as being clearly male or female; other Bodhisattvas are also depicted in some statues with a similar ambiguous gender to indicate that what they represent is beyond all worldly opposites. Statues of another Bodhisattva, Acalanatha, can be rather startling since he is often illustrated in the form of a fierce-looking man holding a sword and rope; he represents the aspect of vigilance and earnest effort, the rope symbolizing willingness to restrain old habits and the sword symbolizing the wise discernment which cuts away delusions. Another commonly seen statue in Mahayana temples is that of Kstigharba, who appears in the form of a simple monk and represents the fact that everyone can find enlightenment. He is sometimes portrayed in a number of different settings, indicating that no matter what a person's circumstances, the Path is always available.

Up to this point in discussing celestial Buddhas and Bodhisattvas, I have referred to them as representing or symbolizing certain things. However, some Buddhists take them to be more than that: for these people, Buddhas and Bodhisattvas are actual beings. As beings, they are thought to reside in various spiritual realms which people cannot see, such as heavens (sometimes called 'deva realms,' 'deva' being a term for gods). And, as individual entities, they can be a source for spiritual assistance, and so they are sometimes prayed to or otherwise asked for their intervention and help. The physical statues, paintings, etcetera, are not prayed to, but the entities which they represent sometimes are.

This, of course, re-opens the question of whether Buddhists believe in God or gods, and it certainly looks a lot like worship in the usual sense of the term. As a matter of fact, there are other Buddhists who feel that this type of practice is going too far afield from the Buddha's original teachings. My own view is that, while this criticism is probably justified in some cases, in many cases it is not. If the forms of any religious practice are simply helpful means of pointing to, and bringing people closer to, spiritual realities which are beyond the scope of those forms, then it becomes apparent that all forms of practice must have both costs and benefits. In the case of the worship of celestial Buddhas and Bodhisattvas, the cost can sometimes be that people become attached to the worship and either lose sight of the larger perspective of the Eightfold Path, begin to attribute unreal magical powers to the object of their devotions, and/or turn their devotional practice into an excuse not to take responsibility for their personal lives.

But for people who avoid these pitfalls, and who happen to be of a devotional nature, the benefits of a worshipful approach can be immense. This type of practice can be a vehicle for deep Buddhist spirituality through encouraging people to give up the self in the service of 'Something Greater' and to transcend the illusion that they know all there is to know.

For example, consider the practice of the Pure Land school of Mahayana Buddhism, which is one of the most worshipful of all Buddhist traditions. Here the trainee is taught to recite the name of the Buddha Amitabha and to have faith that, if he or she truly calls upon that celestial Buddha at the time of death, rebirth will occur in Amitabha's heavenly realm (or Pure Land) where conditions are more favorable for continued progress towards enlightenment. Taken simplistically, this practice can lead to some obvious problems: attributing magical powers to a God-like entity, misunderstanding the teachings on karma or about there being no soul, and avoiding responsibility for personal behavior. And sometimes one does see an adherent of this school act as if he or she can get away with any sort of unethical behavior without consequences, because all that needs to be done is to call upon Amitabha at the end of life and everything will be well. This, however, is a gross abuse of the practice: that's not really what Pure Land Buddhism teaches. More subtle costs occur when followers focus so much upon the devotional aspect that they miss opportunities for ongoing personal spiritual inquiry or for selfless giving to others. But, again, that is not to practice Pure Land Buddhism in the way that is intended.

Although my own school of Buddhism is not Pure Land, I have had the privilege of spending some time in temples of this tradition, and what I have seen among serious and experienced trainees is anything but simplistic and superficial. For them, the recitation of the name of Amitabha can be a profound meditation, and the entire way of practice brings them closer to the whole of the Eightfold Path. For people who respond naturally to a devotional approach, this way provides doors into religious training that many other forms of Buddhism cannot offer.

Similar examples of cost and benefit can be found all throughout Buddhism. As another example, we could look on the opposite side of the spectrum of devotion, at some of the schools which emphasize meditation and individual responsibility, such as within the Theravada family or the Zen schools of the Mahayana family. Here one sometimes encounters followers who practice meditation for purely selfish reasons, seeking to acquire magical psychic powers, and believing that the 'power of their meditation' will overcome their karma and thus allow them, too, to get away with unethical behavior without consequences. Again, what we have is a clear abuse of the practice: none of the meditation schools actually teach anything of the sort, but they are open to being misunderstood in this way. It is kind of interesting, by the way, how people will abuse almost anything in order to justify doing what they please without looking closely at the consequences; fortunately, such intoxicated states of mind are inherently unstable and cannot last forever in the face of how things really work. Serious and experienced followers of the meditation schools find that their practices, like the ones taught by the devotional schools, result in people giving up the self, transcending the illusion that they know all there is to know, gladly walking onward in unknowing, and making their lives into an offering to all beings. Differences between Buddhist schools in the area of devotion and worship, which appear large in theory and which produce quite different types of practice, seem to shrink in significance when we look at their results.

In the process of discussing celestial Buddhas and Bodhisattvas, I have used the terms 'heavens' and 'spiritual realms.' While I'm at it, I may as well throw in the terms 'hells,' 'ghosts,' and 'titans.' If that doesn't make Buddhism sound like a 'good old-fashioned religion,' what would? Well, Buddhists sometimes do use all of those terms, but once again not quite in the way one might think. The historical Buddha mentioned all sorts of unseen spiritual realms such as these (plus some other, totally formless ones), but once again He didn't spend a lot of time talking about them because He didn't regard them as all that important. For the same reason, I am not going to go into detailed descriptions of them. They are simply considered to be alternate realms of reality within a natural universe, places where beings are born and die just as they do on earth. Heavens and hells, for example, are viewed in Buddhism as spiritual worlds in which beings experience great pleasure or pain, respectively. There are a large number of heaven and hell realms mentioned briefly in Buddhist texts, and although their inhabitants are thought of as being very long-lived by human standards, they are not immortal and their place in heaven or hell is not permanent. The same is true of the worlds of the ghosts or the titans ('pretas' and 'asuras' in the Sanskrit language), whose residents experience great unfulfilled longing or anger, respectively.

Some Buddhists speak about these alternate realms of reality and some don't; some believe in their existence as actual places and others see them more as temporary states of mind which people create for themselves in this world. But never are they thought of as eternal reward or punishment, because the principles of change, of no eternal soul, and of no sin (nor eternal judgement) still apply.

Finally, it seems necessary to consider the role of ceremonial in Buddhism, for if the Buddha taught that reliance upon rite and ritual is something that gets in the way, then what legitimate purpose can ceremonies serve in His religion? The answer is very simple: ceremony is another one of those things which, while not necessary for the practice of Buddhism, can nonetheless be very helpful.

There are all manner of Buddhist ceremonies. Some mark the important points in people's lives and help them use those times to rededicate themselves to a higher purpose: ceremonies for the naming of a child, coming of age, marriage, and funeral and memorial ceremonies can serve this purpose. The latter are meant not only to transfer merit for the benefit of any karmic disturbance left behind by the deceased but also to help the living understand and accept the great change which we know as death.

Other ceremonies mark different stages of commitment to religious practice. There are ceremonies in which a person first undertakes to follow the Buddhist Way. In some traditions, other ceremonies mark the deepening commitment of an individual, either as a Buddhist householder or as a monk. For monks, there are also ceremonial confirmations of becoming a full priest, a teacher, etcetera. All of these are helpful in understanding the relevant commitments more deeply and in appreciating the solemnity and significance of taking such steps in the Buddhist Path. This type of ceremony is also of use to others; it identifies people who are qualified to teach and advise them in different ways. All of these forms of ritual help to draw together the followers of each school of Buddhism through shared celebrations of their common heritage.

Still other ceremonies express gratitude and joy for the spiritual ancestors: those who have practiced the Way in ages past and who have passed along their wisdom to the present generation. The greatest of these is called 'Wesak,' and it commemorates the birth, enlightenment, and death of the historical Buddha, Shakyamuni. It is sort of like a Buddhist Christmas and Easter all rolled into one. Wesak is one of the few ceremonies which all Buddhists share in common. Individual schools add other ceremonies in celebration of the births and deaths of their founders or of other great figures in their history. In traditions which revere the celestial Buddhas and Bodhisattvas, many of these have their own festival days, when their particular attributes are called to mind and praised through ritual.

Finally, there are ceremonies which express various aspects of teaching. The precepts are often given in ceremonial form, and meditation frequently has formal, ritual aspects. In some traditions, both teaching and spiritual counseling are done in a ceremonial setting. The ancient Buddhist texts can be recited in special solemn and dignified ways, as can the rules for monastic training, the Bodhisattva Vows, etcetera. In all of these situations, the ceremony serves as a nonverbal way of enriching the meaning of the teaching.

In many Buddhist ceremonies altars are beautifully decorated, incense is burnt, candles or lanterns are lit, and offerings of food or other items are made. People gather together and chant the ancient verses and scriptures, often led by one or more monks or priests, who may be dressed in vestments which range from extremely plain to highly ornate. The purpose of all of this is to communicate something to people—to inspire, to educate, to express a shared feeling or commitment—in a way that is appropriate to the particular purpose of the ceremony. While these ceremonies clearly involve the use of 'rite and ritual,' they are not contrary to the Buddha's admonition since they do not instill a sense of *reliance* upon that rite and ritual. To use ceremonial to *offer* something (teaching, gratitude, or an expression of joy, for instance) is quite different than to use ceremonial to *seek to get* something (like good luck, health, wealth, or favorable rebirths).

The physical offerings placed upon a Buddhist altar are regarded simply as outpourings of joy and gratitude; in that spirit, they are accepted by the monks or given to the poor. There is no belief that the ceremony mystically transforms them into something else which will bestow special benefits upon the giver. Food may be placed at the feet of a statue of a celestial Bodhisattva, for example, but the donor is under no illusions that this food will somehow be spiritually consumed by that being, who will then become favorably disposed towards the wishes of the person who made the offering. To make any offering freely from one's heart, with no expectations, is a beneficial thing, and so the giving of offerings does have the effect of creating merit (positive karma), and merit in turn will have its good effects upon the donor and others. This is in accord with the Way. On the other hand, to give offerings, attend ceremonies, etcetera, with the deliberate intention of creating merit and of getting a reward, in a sort of 'spiritual economy,' is obviously a selfish act, and it therefore creates negative karma instead of merit. Merit is like that: try to hold onto it and it slips out of your grasp, but give it away freely and it returns a hundred-fold.

Ceremonial, like the other forms of religious practice, has its costs and benefits. The benefits have been mentioned above, and for some people they are quite considerable. For them, ceremonial can be meditation in action, or it can be a doorway into experiencing Buddhist teachings in a way which words simply cannot convey. But what of the costs? For other people, ceremony simply fails to communicate what is intended, and for them there seems little point to it. That need not be a problem, since attending ceremonies is not a requirement in most schools of Buddhism, and since there is merit in participating in ceremonies for the benefit of others, even if those ceremonies don't particularly inspire one.

The only serious cost of ceremonial occurs when it is taken simplistically and magically, when the Buddha's warning not to place reliance upon it is ignored. For example, you sometimes find Buddhists making lavish offerings at funerals, way beyond the limits of their financial means, in the belief that those offerings will be transformed magically into something that will benefit their deceased relatives. In some Buddhist countries, the sons and daughters of a dead couple may save money for decades in order to pay for one grand memorial ceremony for their dead parents, at the climax of which a huge paper palace (complete with working miniature electric lights and paper servants, a paper Mercedes parked outside) is burned as an offering, in the belief that the parents will then be able to live in luxury in a heavenly realm. This is ceremonial gone astray, and the monks shake their heads sadly at such displays. In the short term, some people may find that reliance upon such things gives more comfort than acceptance of what their religion actually teaches them. However, in the long term, such magical views of the universe are unstable and do not last. So, the monks are patient. They gently guide people away from such things while not insisting; they trust that, with time, the practice of the Eightfold Path will have its effects.

This gentle and patient approach is not a bad model for any Buddhist to adopt in his or her relation to Buddhism as a whole. If an individual approaches things in this way, it may not matter whether ceremony is thought of as being worship nor if Buddhism is called a religion. In the rest of this book, I have referred to it as a religion because scholars generally classify it that way and because that is how I, myself, view it. But since Buddhism is a thing that is *lived*, that is *done* in daily life, then the practice of it is more important than the words or ideas that are used to describe it. Taken in this way, the questions which arise about Buddhism as a religion can be a form of the productive doubt which invites people onwards, regardless of their current viewpoint on such things. Taken in the opposite way, as decisions which we require ourselves to make about 'how things must be,' the same questions can lead to a hardening of positions and to fruitless arguments. And one of the things which the Buddha's disciples found out was that, if there is an argument, it cannot be about truth. Truths, in Buddhism, do not insist loudly upon themselves.

7.
How to Find Out More

This chapter is for people who would like to find out more: it contains material designed to help you search for more information about some of the topics that have been mentioned, how to locate a Buddhist temple or practice group, and some advice on how to find a personal teacher. Fine scholarly bibliographies and current guides to Buddhist groups already exist, so there is no point to repeating that sort of information here. Instead, I will simply offer some lists of 'key words': words that relate to things that have been explored in this book and which might be useful in searching for more details. The main places to use these key words would be literature searches in libraries or search engines on the Internet. In either case, the key words provided below should be enough to get a person started. Have fun!

Information

If you are looking for more information about various aspects of Buddhism, try searching under some of the following words. When the tables below say 'use additional words,' it means that if you just use this one key word you are likely to get too many references, so it might be better to narrow your search by adding additional key words. Terms which appear in **bold** in the 'explanation' section of this table (and of the one which follows) are other key words found in this table; those which appear in *italics* are key words in the table on how to locate a temple or practice group; and those which are in ***bold italics*** are found in both places. The page numbers refer to where the term, or a related concept, appears in this book. You might find useful details by looking at these words not only in English but also in the languages from which Buddhism has come to the West. For this reason, translations of some of the key words are given in parentheses, with a letter indicating the language from which the translation comes: 'C' for Chinese, 'J' for Japanese, 'P' for Pali, 'S' for Sanskrit, and 'T' for Tibetan.

Term	Explanation	Page #s
Amitabha	(C: O-mi-t'o-fo; J: Amida; T: 'Od-dpag-tu-med-pa) in ***Mahayana Buddhism***, the **Buddha** of Infinite Light; the primary Buddha of *Pure Land* Buddhism.	53, 117–120
anatta	(S: anatman) the basic principle that there is no separate self or soul.	74–81, 91–92
anicca	(S: anitya) the basic law of change within the universe.	4–5, 9–10, 25, 42, 69–72, 79
arahant	(S: arhat or arhant; C: lo-han; J: arakan; T: skyes-mchog) one who has dropped all attachments and found **nirvana.**	31–32, 138
Avalokitesvara	(C: Kuan-yin or Kuan-shih-yin; J: Kanzeon or Kannon;	117–118

Term	Explanation	Page #s
Avalokitesvara (*continued*)	T: sPyan-ras-gzigs-dbang-phyug) in **Mahayana Buddhism**, the **Bodhisattva** of Great Compassion.	
Bodhisattva; bodhisattva	(C: Pu-sa; J: Bosatsu; T: byang-chub-sems-dpa') in **Mahayana Buddhism**, an embodiment of a specific aspect of **Buddha Nature**. In lower case, any person on the Path to **enlightenment**. Use additional words.	53, 94, 116–123
Buddha	(C: Fo; J: Butsu; T: Sangs-rgyas) the historical founder of **Buddhism**; one of the embodiments of the **Buddha Nature** in **Mahayana Buddhism**. Use additional words.	53, 55, 63, 80, 103–125, 137
Buddha Nature	(S: Buddhata; C: Fo-hsing; J: Bussho; T: de-bzhin-bshegs-pa'i-snying-po) in **Mahayana Buddhism**, the essential **enlightenment** of the universe and all people.	35–36, 55, 79, 117
Buddhism	the general name of the religion. There are two (or three) basic types: **Mahayana** and **Theravada** (and, in some systems, **Vajrayana**). Use additional words.	References found throughout the book
dependent origination	also 'conditioned coproduction' (P: paticca samupada) the relationship of attachment, perception, and delusion.	30

Term	Explanation	Page #s
Dharma or Dhamma	(C: Fa; J: Ho; T: chos) the teachings of **Buddha**s and spiritual ancestors. Use additional words.	36, 55
dukkha	(S: duhkha) the first **Noble Truth**, that our usual way of living entails inherent unhappiness and dissatisfaction.	5–8, 11–12, 77–78
Eightfold Path	the fourth **Noble Truth**; the Way to **enlightenment** through religious practice in daily life.	27–67, 83, 104, 136
enlightenment	(S: bodhi) full oneness with the truth, complete non-attachment; when continuous, called **nirvana**. Use additional words.	29–43, 47–48, 73–74, 88–98, 114–115
Four Noble Truths	the founding principles of **Buddhism**.	32–34, 69, 72
karma or kamma	the third **niyama**, or law of the universe; the causal link between action and its resulting sensation. Use additional words.	86–98, 119, 123–124
Mahayana	the 'Great Vehicle'; one of the two (or three) main families of **Buddhism**, the other being the **Theravada** (and sometimes the **Vajrayana**). Use additional words.	94, 117–120
Maitreya	(C: Mi-le; J: Miroku; T: Byams-pa) in **Mahayana Buddhism**, the **Buddha** who is to come in the future.	116

Term	Explanation	Page #s
Manjusri or Manjushri	(C: Wen-shu-shih-l; J: Monju; T: 'Jan-dpal) in *Mahayana Buddhism*, the **Bodhisattva** of Great Wisdom.	53, 117
meditation	one of the aspects of the **Eightfold Path**, involving both concentration and insight. Use additional words.	10, 36–37, 62–67, 114, 120, 124
nirvana or nibbana	living within continuous **enlightenment**; the result of complete non-attachment. Use additional words.	31, 73, 79, 94, 101–102, 114–115
niyamas	the five fundamental Buddhist laws of the universe.	83–98
Prajnaparamita	in *Mahayana Buddhism*, the **Bodhisattva** embodying the Perfection of Wisdom; also a major text on wisdom.	53, 117
Samantabhadra	(C: P'u-hsieh; J: Fugen; T: Gun-du-bzang-po) in *Mahayana Buddhism*, the **Bodhisattva** embodying Loving Patience.	117
sangha	the four-fold community of committed Buddhists, including both ordained and lay people, women and men.	55–56
Shakyamuni	the name of the historical **Buddha**, founder of the religion, who lived in the sixth century B.C.E.	105–117, 122

Term	Explanation	Page #s
Theravada	the 'Vehicle of the Elders'; one of the two (or three) main families of **Buddhism**, the other being the **Mahayana** (and, in some systems, the **Vajrayana**).	94, 120
Vairocana or Vairochana	(C: P'i-lu-she-na or Ta-ji Ju-lai; J: Roshana Butsu or Dainichi Nyorai; T: Kun-rigs-rnam-par-snang-mdzad) in **Mahayana Buddhism**, the Cosmic **Buddha**; the embodiment of Truth or of the Universe Itself.	117
Vajrayana	the 'Diamond Vehicle'; the Way of Tibetan Buddhism, sometimes considered as part of the **Mahayana** family, sometimes as a separate family of its own.	

A Temple or Practice Group

To make contact with a Buddhist temple or practice group in your area, try looking in a Buddhist directory, examining the telephone book, or searching the Internet using some of the following key words. It may also help to look under the foreign words given in parentheses. Some temples and groups can also be found by looking for their announcements in the local newspaper or their fliers in libraries, community centers, bookstores, or vegetarian food stores.

Term	Explanation	Page #s
Buddhism	Use with additional words found below, or with country names such as Burmese, Cambodian, Chinese, Japanese, Korean, Laotian, Sri Lankan, Thai, *Tibetan*, or Vietnamese. Also try variants such as 'Buddhist.'	References found throughout the book
Gelugpa	a school of the *Tibetan* branch of **Buddhism**.	
Kagyu	a school of the *Tibetan* branch of **Buddhism**.	
Mahayana	the family of **Buddhism** which is primarily practiced in Tibet, China, Korea, and Japan. Use additional words.	94, 117–120
meditation	the practice of concentration and insight, most emphasized by the **Theravada**, *Tibetan*, and *Zen* schools. Use additional words.	10, 36–37, 62–67, 114, 120, 124
Nyingma	a school of the *Tibetan* branch of **Buddhism**.	
Pure Land	(C: Shin; J: Jodo Shin) a branch of **Mahayana Buddhism** which emphasizes devotion to **Amitabha Buddha**.	119–120
Rinzai	(C: Lin-chi) a school of *Zen* which emphasizes **meditation** and intuitive study of ancient stories of **enlightenment** ('koans').	

Term	Explanation	Page #s
Sakya	a school of the *Tibetan* branch of **Buddhism**.	
Soto	(C: Ts'ao-Tung) a school of *Zen* which emphasizes **meditation**, mindful work, and precepts.	43, 58, 64
Theravada	the family of **Buddhism** which is practiced primarily in Sri Lanka and Southeast Asia. It emphasizes **meditation**, study of the ancient texts, and precepts.	94, 120
Tibetan	the **Vajrayana** schools of **Buddhism** practiced in Tibet, including *Gelugpa*, *Kagyu*, *Nyingma*, and *Sakya*. They emphasize **meditation**, textual study, and ceremony.	46, 105
Vajrayana	the esoteric family of **Buddhism**. It is practiced mainly in Tibet, with some forms also found in China and Japan.	
Vipassana	'Insight Meditation': a lay **meditation** movement associated with the **Theravada** family of **Buddhism**.	
Zen	(S: Dhyana; C: Ch'an) a branch of **Mahayana Buddhism** which is practiced primarily in China, Korea, Vietnam, and Japan; it emphasizes **meditation.** See *Soto* and *Rinzai*.	36, 43, 58, 64, 71, 94, 120

Most temples are quite glad to give people a tour and to answer questions about their particular form of Buddhist practice. If your interest extends beyond simple information and you are looking for a possible place to study Buddhism yourself, then a good next step might be to spend a bit of time joining in the practice at each of the temples or groups that you have located and see how things feel to you. Finding a Buddhist tradition and place of practice to which a person can make a commitment is largely an intuitive thing; so, while I will give some tips on possible things to look for, there is no substitute for simply going to a place a few times, attending some religious activities, and getting the feel of things. If a person feels very much at home, that is a good sign. Oddly enough, if one feels both strongly attracted to the place and at the same time scared, that is also a good sign. This mixed feeling often means that a part of you recognizes that the teaching or the group is right, while another part is frightened of the challenge which this presents. On the other hand, if you feel uneasy about the place or the people, if the whole thing seems irrelevant, or if it is somehow just 'wrong,' then you might want to look elsewhere.

In addition to these gut-level indicators, here are some rational ones which you can use as well. Is the group part of a larger organization, or does it stand completely alone? Being part of something larger doesn't necessarily mean that it is better, but small and alone tends to be unstable. Is it, and/or its larger organization recognized by some association of other Buddhists? While such recognition cannot guarantee high standards of ethics and quality teaching, it does suggest that other people who should know about these things have a reasonable degree of confidence in the group. Speaking of ethics, does the group have any explicit ethical guidelines, rules of conduct, etcetera, for its members and its teachers? Is the temple or group recognized by the government as a legitimate charity, religious non-profit corporation, tax-exempt trust, or similar entity? Do you feel that the group is pressuring you to join? Such pressure would be unusual in Buddhism, as the general thrust of Buddhist teaching runs towards individual responsibility and the exercise of free will. If you feel pressured, it might mean that something is not quite right.

A Teacher

For the person who wishes to become a serious practicing Buddhist, some sort of teaching relationship is advisable. The types of relationship will vary widely with different schools of Buddhism and even across different groups within a given school. They can include intensely personal, life long, one-to-one connections, very flexible study with a number of teachers, informal associations with other students in the group who are simply a little more experienced, and formal and impersonal teaching done in large groups at infrequent intervals. Nonetheless, having at least one live person, from whom one can hear advice and to whom one can go with questions, is important. This is because the words used to describe Buddhist principles are very approximate, and also because some of the aspects of the Eightfold Path (particularly the ones relating to mindfulness and meditation) have to be learned by a certain amount of trial and error. Books, no matter how good, can get a person only so far.

How does one find such a teaching relationship? First, you have to find a suitable temple or practice group, since that is where teachers are usually located. As with finding a group, finding a teacher or teachers is largely a matter of what feels right. All of what was said about the intuitive side of locating a suitable place of practice also applies to locating a suitable person to guide that practice. In addition, here are some other questions to consider. Who was the teacher's teacher? Buddhism has been around for a very long time and its teachers are usually members of long lineages. A teacher who did not study with, and was not certified by, their own teacher is far less apt to be reliable than one who did. How long did the teachers you have found spend in religious study before starting out to teach on their own, what levels of certification do they hold within their organizations, and how long have they been teaching? As in any profession, experience and level of training may not guarantee excellence, but 'more' is generally better than 'less.' The question of whether the teacher is ordained is a bit tricky, as some schools of Buddhism have lineages of excellent lay teachers, others give ordination only after a great deal of teaching experience, and yet others require ordination before even starting to train someone as a teacher. Nonetheless, ordination is a meaningful concept in most types of Buddhism, and it is worth asking about what it means in the tradition you have encountered and where the teacher stands in respect to it. If ordained, has the person vowed to follow certain rules and precepts; if not, is he or she subject to some other set of ethical guidelines?

One of the most fruitful areas to examine with regard to a teacher is the state of his or her students. After all, as my own teacher pointed out to me when I first thought of studying with her, the teacher is the 'product' of study and practice under a previous teacher, and that earlier teacher is not the one you are thinking of studying with. So, it is your fellow students who can show you what to expect as a result of studying with the teacher at hand. Are they becoming as you would wish to be? It takes a bit of time to get a sense of how that question is being answered, but it may be the most important question to consider. All of the other questions mentioned above might be helpful, but they're a bit theoretical; this one goes to the heart of the matter. It goes right back to the advice that the Buddha gave to those village elders long ago: discern the wisdom of a teacher by the actual effects of his or her teaching on real people. Each of us is different, of course, and there is no guarantee that the effects would be similar for you, because, among other things, a whole lot depends on what you do with that teaching. Yet, if you feel that most of the students are moving in a direction that you would like to go in, that is a very good sign.

While waiting for such a feeling to develop over time, there is another question that is worth asking. Are the students or group members nice; are they normal? Are they 'regular people,' 'good folks,' or is there something a little odd, cold, self-important, or even creepy about them? The latter signs do not speak well of their teacher, since Buddhism, when properly taught, cuts away at the roots of the things that make people strange, aloof, proud, etcetera. What typically arises when these roots are cut is a warmth, gentleness, generosity, empathy, and genuineness that make someone a pleasure to be around. These qualities are the only outward signs of enlightenment, and they are a long way from the penetrating stares, self-important speeches, demonstrations of personal or psychic power, and other magic tricks which the misguided occasionally come up with.

One final word of advice to the person who wants to take Buddhism all the way. Once you have found a suitable tradition, group, and teacher, *stay with them*. Things will not always go well, and not everything will please you or be as you think it should be. That is inevitable for two reasons. First, because each of us brings to Buddhist training our own set of attachments and delusions, they are bound to 'rub the wrong way' against parts of a genuine practice. Second, even the best teacher and group are human and they will make mistakes from time to time. The fact that they sometimes 'mess things up' does not mean that they are unworthy of being your teacher and fellow students: it simply means that their personal training is ongoing. Since enlightenment is not a finished thing but rather an ongoing process, and since even the continuous enlightenment of the arahant does not confer omniscience or infallibility, mistakes are going to be made. If seekers after Buddha's Way require that their teachers or religious groups meet the ideals floating around inside their own heads, they will never find what they are looking for.

The same is true if one goes from teacher to teacher, group to group, tradition to tradition, sampling what is offered by each and then putting them together into one's own personal mixture. This is tempting, but it guarantees frustration. The first reason has already been mentioned above: it's the 'prickly bits' from which we sometimes learn the most. If an individual picks and chooses only the parts of various teachings which he or she likes, the most useful parts will tend to be left out, and the person will be apt to stagnate.

Second, the existing traditions of Buddhist practice have evolved into their present forms over hundreds, often thousands, of years. That process has distilled the wisdom of many generations of sincere people seeking after truth. Why would one deliberately ignore the assistance which they have so kindly offered to us and insist upon 're-inventing the wheel' by creating a new form of practice?

Are there some imperfections in those traditions? Of course there are; it seems that this is true of all religious traditions, Buddhist and non-Buddhist alike. And I suspect that, by setting aside our personal ideas of perfection, committing ourselves to a particular religion wholeheartedly, and doing the very best training we can within that tradition—with its imperfections alongside its wisdom—each of us unknowingly joins in the age-old process of improving both our own religion and ourself. Perhaps, in this way, all humankind moves just a little closer to truth. At least, that's how it looks from within this Buddhist.

About the Author

Rev. Daizui MacPhillamy is a Buddhist priest and teacher in the Order of Buddhist Contemplatives, a Western monastic order within the Soto Zen tradition. He was ordained in 1973, at the age of twenty-eight, by Rev. Master Jiyu-Kennett, one of the first Western female Roshis, or Zen Masters. She, in turn, was a disciple of the late Keido Chisan Koho, Zenji, abbot of one of the two main training monasteries of the Soto school in Japan. Rev. MacPhillamy studied with his master at Shasta Abbey, a seminary of the Order in northern California, until her death in 1996. For the last twenty-one years of this time, he served as her personal assistant. Over the course of his monastic training, he received Dharma Transmission from Rev. Master Jiyu-Kennett, and he was named by her as a Master and Dharma Heir. Upon her death, Rev. MacPhillamy was elected to succeed her as Head of the Order, a position which he continues to hold. In addition to serving in this capacity, he also acts as Prior of a small mountain temple, the Fugen Forest Hermitage, in northwestern California, and he functions as editor both for the publication of the oral teachings of his master and for the Shasta Abbey Press translations of classic Zen Buddhist texts.

The Order of Buddhist Contemplatives is the lineage family association for the disciples and descendants of Rev. Master Jiyu-Kennett. There are about one hundred women and men who are monastic members of the Order, serving temples and meditation groups in Canada, Germany, the Netherlands, the United Kingdom, and the United States. Further information about the Order and its activities can be found on the world wide web at: *http://www.obcon.org.*

Notes

Notes

Notes

Notes